Kid's Decor

Courtesy of Vermont Tubbs, Inc.

Courtesy of The Glidden Company

Courtesy of Fashion Bed Group

Courtesy of Eisenhart Wallcoverings Co.

Courtesy of What's A Mother To Do?

Courtesy of What's A Mother To Do?

Dedication

Library of Congress Cataloging-in-Publication Data

Skinner, Tina.
Kid's decor : interior inspirations : infants through teens / by Tina Skinner.
p. cm.
ISBN 0-7643-1613-3 (paperback)
1. Children's rooms. 2. Interior decoration. I. Title.
NK2117.C4 S58 2002
747.7'7--dc21
2002001588

Copyright © 2002 by Schiffer Publishing, Ltd.

All rights reserved. No part of this work may be reproduced or used in any form or by any means—graphic, electronic, or mechanical, including photocopying or information storage and retrieval systems—without written permission from the copyright holder.
"Schiffer," "Schiffer Publishing Ltd. & Design," and the "Design of pen and ink well" are registered trademarks of Schiffer Publishing Ltd.

Designed by Bonnie M. Hensley
Cover design by Bruce M. Waters
Type set in Kids/Lydian BT

ISBN: 0-7643-1613-3
Printed in Hong Kong

Published by Schiffer Publishing Ltd.
4880 Lower Valley Road
Atglen, PA 19310
Phone: (610) 593-1777; Fax: (610) 593-2002
E-mail: Schifferbk@aol.com
Please visit our web site catalog at www.schifferbooks.com
We are always looking for people to write books on new and related subjects. If you have an idea for a book please contact us at the above address.

This book may be purchased from the publisher. Include $3.95 for shipping. Please try your bookstore first. You may write for a free catalog.

In Europe, Schiffer books are distributed by
Bushwood Books
6 Marksbury Ave.
Kew Gardens
Surrey TW9 4JF England
Phone: 44 (0) 20 8392-8585; Fax: 44 (0) 20 8392-9876
E-mail: Bushwd@aol.com
Free postage in the U.K., Europe; air mail at cost.

Courtesy of Eisenhart Wallcoverings Co.

Contents

Courtesy of The Glidden Company

Introduction — 8

Step-by-Step Rooms - Great project ideas you can do yourself — 16

Princess Room — 17

Jungle Room — 22

Formula One Room — 27

Bringing Baby Home - Create first memories for your new creation — 30

His Room - Ideas he'll approve of — 48

Her Room - Ideas she'll insist on — 82

You're Always Welcome - Hosting young guests, and welcoming grown ones home — 121

Weekend Retreats - Great ideas for that second home — 130

Playrooms - Room to romp, pretend, and prepare — 136

Resource Guide - Here's where to get great stuff — 143

Courtesy of P.J. Kids

Courtesy of Eisenhart Wallcoverings Co.

Courtesy of Eisenhart Wallcoverings Co.

Introduction

I've got one – an adorable and completely indulged little girl. I want the world for her. She's royalty in my eyes, a princess worthy of everything pretty, and deserving of everything fun.

Within budget, what parent doesn't want to pamper and please a child? Who doesn't want to provide a child with a room they love, where they go to play, to study, and most importantly, to rest peacefully and enjoy happy dreams?

Here's a book packed with ideas for every child and every home. Whether you're working with a tiny loft, or have space to branch out and create a playroom in addition to the sleeping quarters there are ideas here for you. This book is a wonderful tool for you and your child.

I recommend that you plan a few family meetings – husband and wife if you're welcoming home your first; mom, dad, and child if your young one is old enough to participate. You might be surprised at how early on your toddler can express preferences, and the visuals in this book will help enhance their ability to tell you how they feel. Make sure you have Post-it® tabs on hand to mark your favorite pages. And make notes on those tabs, recording what is liked about the room shown, and what is not. Ask lots of questions. What bed style do you like best? How about the dressers and armoires? Do you like color on the walls, or splashed on the textiles, or both? What color schemes appeal? Ask them to find favorite colors in clothing, candy, and toys, then put them side by side to see which look best together. Then pick two dominant colors, one or two accent colors.

If budget is a consideration, you need to discuss this up front with children old enough

Accessories accessorize a bed, in a girlish theme that delights the occupant. Courtesy of California Kids

to understand. If they fall in love with something that goes beyond the bounds of that budget, you'll need to hunt for comparable, but less expensive, alternatives.

With younger children, you don't want to approach this book with "what do you want?" questions. Rather, ask them what they like, learn what's important to them, and then surprise them with what you can provide.

You'll also want to look for rooms with similar configurations – size, door, and window locations, and study how the furnishings were arranged within. Another great exercise is to do a scale drawing of your room on graph paper; measure and mark out a floor plan. Use a separate piece of graph paper and cut out scale blocks to represent the bed, a dresser, a desk and chair, and move these about on the floor plan. Add some color and some block letters and even a toddler enjoys this little exercise.

While you're in the planning stages, be sure to talk about the future. Children's tastes change as quickly as the television channels. Explain that, once painted or papered, once the furniture is bought, these are decisions they will live with for many years to come. This is something to keep in mind when discussing that hot pink wall.

Maybe a pillow in that color would be a better choice. Or we might want to consider limiting our Pokémon display to a bulletin board where a collection of trading cards can be displayed, and later replaced with the next collection. Beyond the furnishings, maybe your family moves often. It's important to explain why a seven-foot-long dresser/vanity unit isn't practical, as there might not be room for it in the next home.

When it comes time to shop, or to paint/wallpaper/position art, try to include your child in the process as much as possible. Even young children can assist in many ways that make them feel proud of the finished product. They might be assigned a small block of wall, heavily fortified with drop cloths and protective clothing. Or they might simply be brought in after the painting is finished to help remove tapes used to block off molding or decorative effects. They might help position border papers, and their opinion should certainly be sought when hanging artworks or positioning displays.

By being involved in the planning and execution of their room design, children are able to develop a greater respect for the space. It's more likely, in other words, that they won't be throwing clothes on the floor or using magic marker on the walls. The goal, of course, is a room where your child feels happy and comfortable. Maybe when you suggest "go to your room," it won't be a punishment, but a pleasure.

One far-sighted solution to accommodating a child is to start off with a crib he or she can sleep in all their lives. Here is a wonderful example of a crib that converts into a day bed and a full-size bed. *Courtesy of Berg Furniture*

Bedroom sets are available that move through every stage of life, from crib for an infant, to daybed for a toddler, to big bed for a young adult, then back to daybed for seating in a new apartment, and crib again when the next generation arrives. *Courtesy of Bassett Furniture*

Stackable twins are a wonderful option as the family, or the home, changes. *Courtesy of Vermont Tubbs, Inc.*

If you might move, or if the children might, one consideration is stackable bunk beds that convert into twins. The possibilities are endless for all space requirements. *Courtesy of Berg Furniture*

A rollout desk can be tucked under the bed when not in use. Likewise, a three-drawer dresser can stand alone, or bunk below. Other options include incorporating a bed, or shelving, underneath. *Courtesy of Sandberg Furniture*

Step-by-Step Rooms

Here are a few inspiring projects designed for the do-it-yourselfer. Make a castle for your princess or indulge racecar fantasies for a little boy. A jungle room would be a hit with any animal lover. The projects were designed for beginners and require only the most rudimentary carpentry skills. If you have any questions or run into any obstacles, help is available at your local hardware store or lumberyard, where professionals are paid to offer their experitse. Read all the instructions first so that you can ask any questions you might have initially when you go out to purchase tools and materials.

Remember, safety comes first. The use of standard safety equipment reflects good common sense. Eye protection, a dust mask, and gloves should be used when sawing or machining any type of building material. Neither Schiffer Publishing, Ltd. or Georgia-Pacific Corporation make any warranties expressed or implied regarding these plans, and specifically disclaim the warranties of merchant-ability and fitness for a particular purpose.

Courtesy of Georgia-Pacific

Princess Room

Starting with a sky blue background, layers of molding were built up to create a royal fantasy in this room. Following are basic instructions, created by Georgia-Pacific, to help you create your own fairytale castle. You can vary this design to suit yourself, and personalize it with colors that match your highness's tastes.

Materials Needed

WM 47 crown molding [11/16" x 4-5/8" x room measurements]
WM 273 picture mold [11/16" x 1-3/4" x as desired]
WM 300 chair rail [1-1/16" x 3" x room measurements]
WM 634 [1/2" x 3"] or 622 base [9/16" x 3-1/2"] based on room measurements

Trees:
WM 138 [5/16" x 5/8"], 137 shelf edge [3/8" x 3/4" x 130"], or 135 flat astragal [7/16" x 3/4" x 13']

Castle Headboard:
WM 164 base cap [11/16" x 1-1/8" x 34']
WM 60 crown [9/16" x 1-3/4" x 6']
WM 52 crown [9/16" x 2-3/4" x 14'] or WM 70 bed mold [9/16" x 2-3/4" x 14']
WM 634 base [1/2" x 3" x 14'] (castle towers)
WM 473 casing [9/16" x 2-1/4" x 13']
WM 254 S4S [1/2" x 3/4" x 3']
WM 100 cove [11/16" x 11/16" x 3']
WM 123 half round [5/16" x 5/8" x3']
WM 233 full round [1-5/16" x 1']
WM 248 S4S [3/4" x 1-3/4" x 15']

Other:
Wood paneling or plank paneling
Styrofoam cones and wooden curtain rod
3/4" plywood for headboard, 4' x 8' sheet
Latex flat and semi-gloss enamel
Medium oak wood stain
3d and 4d finish nails
Hammer
Wood glue
Tape measure (preferably 25' rule)
Goggles
Construction paper or fabric for flags
Bandsaw or jigsaw

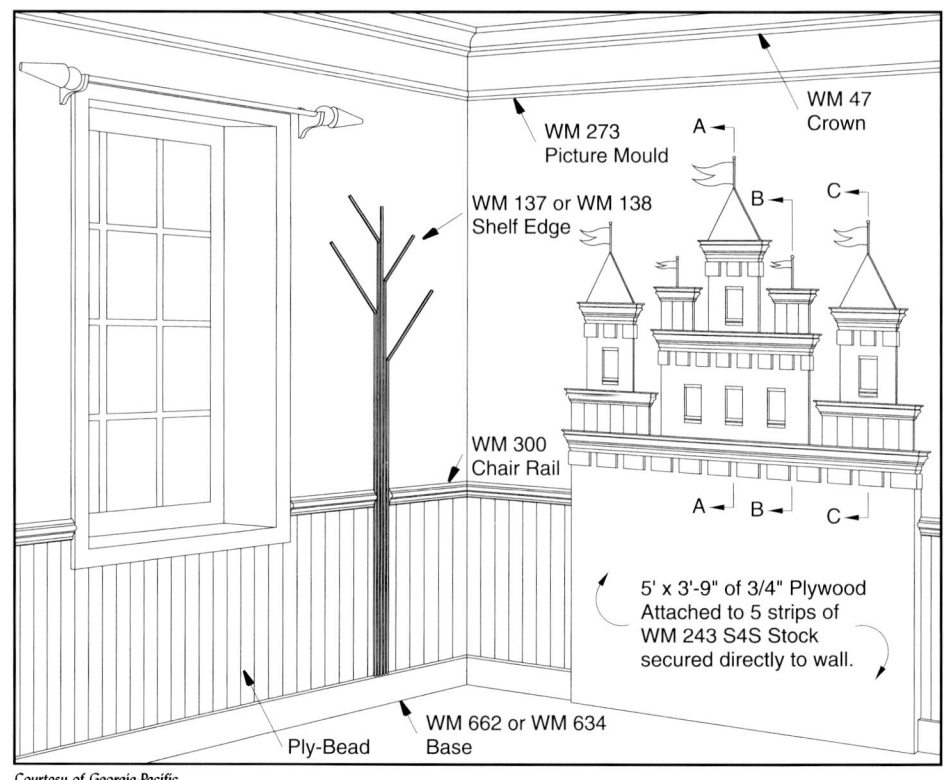

Courtesy of Georgia-Pacific

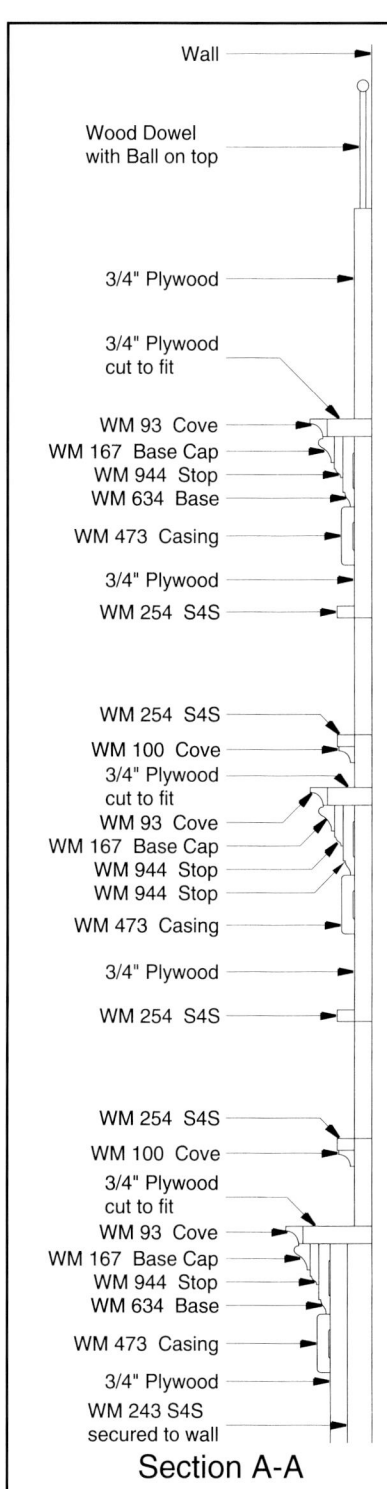

Section A-A

Courtesy of Georgia-Pacific

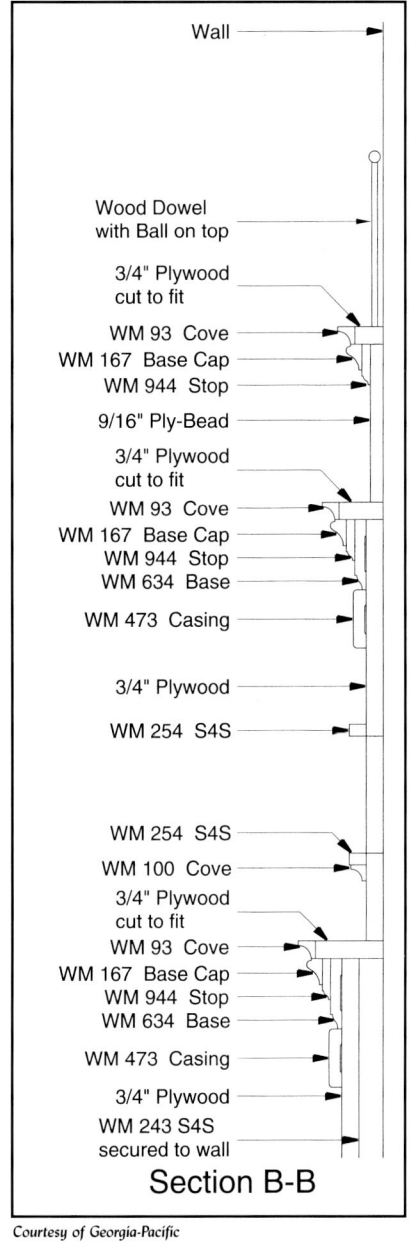

Section B-B

Courtesy of Georgia-Pacific

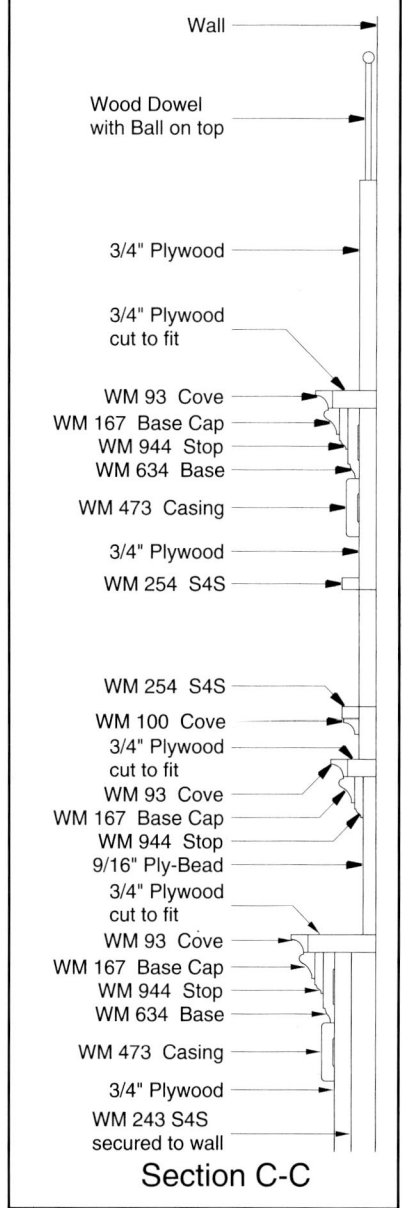

Section C-C

Courtesy of Georgia-Pacific

> Note: It is not necessary to use the exact molding profile indicated. Alternate molding profiles may be substituted at your discretion. Check with your molding retailer to make certain that the substitute casing, base, or other molding profile you choose has dimensions close to those specified above.

19

The Trees of the Enchanted Forest

To create each tree in the enchanted forest, stain four pieces of shelf edge or flat astragal molding (such as WM 138, WM 137 or WM 135) a medium oak finish. Cut molding in lengths varying from 6' to 4' for each tree. Beginning at the base molding, attach the pieces for each tree to the wall with finish nails or glue. Gaps must be left in the chair rail molding to accommodate installing the trees. Then apply molding like branches stemming out from the tree trunk. Using two different size leaf patterns, sponge a variety of the leaves on the wall with matte finish latex. You can cut leaf patterns from an ordinary household sponge, or purchase a stencil from your local craft store. For the best effect, experiment on paper before you begin sponging.

The Curtain Rod

Use a round wooden rod with ball-type finials and then add Styrofoam cones onto the end, painted pink.

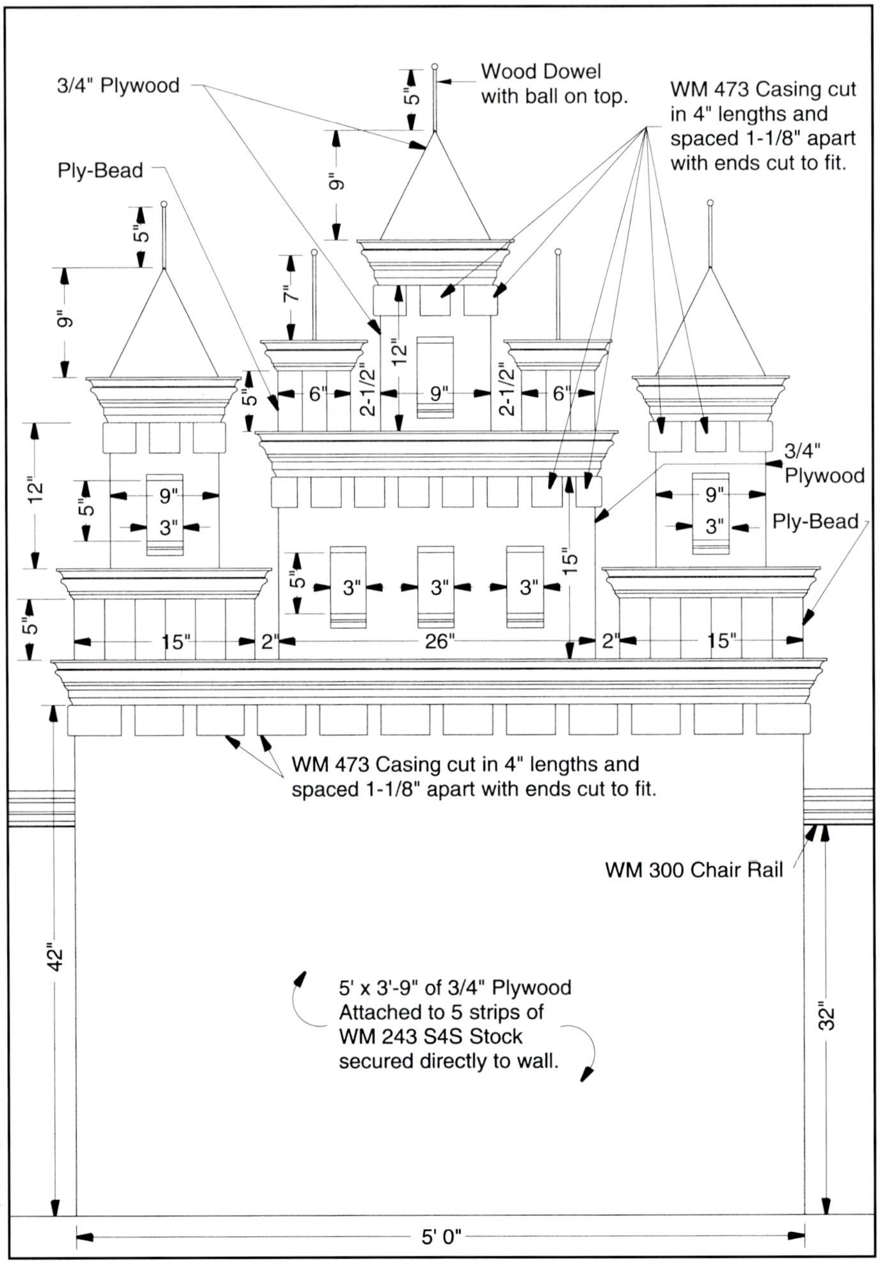

Courtesy of Georgia-Pacific

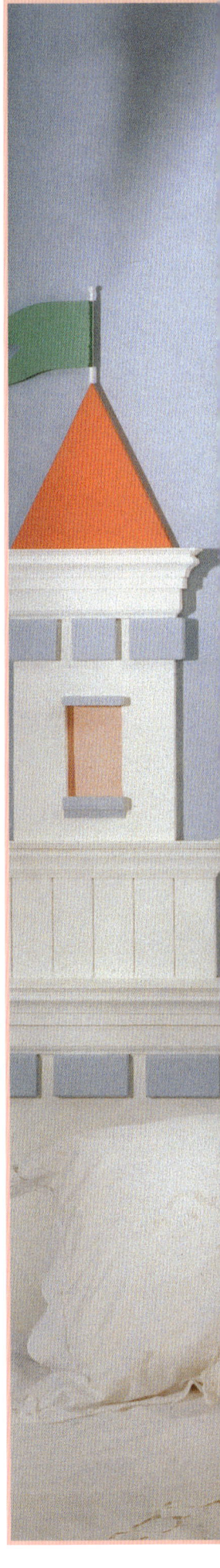

Cut, prime, and paint all the parts of the headboard before constructing. The headboard is made with a 3'9" x 5' piece of 3/4" plywood. Attach five strips of S4S WM 248 to the wall (one for either end of the headboard and three in the middle). Secure the plywood headboard to the S4S so that the headboard sits 1-1/4" out from the wall. Molding is applied to the top. Cut twelve 4" x 2-1/4" squares out of casing (WM 473) and space them evenly underneath the molding. The center part of the castle is made with a 2'2" x 1'3" piece of 3/4" plywood attached directly to the wall. Moldings and 4" x 2-1/2" squares are applied at the top directly to the wall, as in the drawing. The windows are created either by gluing 3" x 5" pieces of S4S stock to the plywood or by cutting 3" x 5" "windows in the plywood with a jigsaw. The top of the window is trimmed in WM 254 S4S and the bottom of the window has a piece of WM 254 SRS with WM 100 cove underneath.

The two castle towers to each side of the center are made with Ply-Bead®. They are 1'3" x 5" and they are spaced 2" from the center piece. They are capped with the same molding as used on the center of the castle, applied directly to the wall.

The three towers with the inverted cones on top are 9" wide and 12" high. The towers and the cones are cut from 3/4" plywood. The cones can be made by scribing a triangle onto the plywood, beginning with a 9-1/2" base, and cutting with a jigsaw or bandsaw. The windows and molding on the three towers are constructed the same way as those on the center piece.

The Little Flagpoles

The little flagpoles are made of WM 123 half rounds (wood dowels), which are notched and glued onto the castle towers of the headboard. Cut crosswise a piece of WM 233 full round to make the ball finial on the flagpole. You can make slip-on fabric flags or glue on construction paper ones. As an option, flags could be changed with the seasons or holidays. These are excellent projects for the resident!

Jungle Room

This room has a 9-foot ceiling and a double bed, but you can easily adjust the materials to accommodate the dimensions of your child's room. Animal posters can be found at the zoo, in a poster or frame shop, or a retail store.

Courtesy of Georgia-Pacific

Materials Needed

WM 248 S4S [3/4" x 1-3/4" x size of poster]
WM 433 casing [9/16" x 3-1/4" x size of poster]
WM 134 flat astragal [11/16" x 1-3/8"] as desired
WM 163 base cap [11/16" x 1-3/8"] as desired
WM 183 panel molding [9/16" x 1-1/8"] as desired
WM 120 half round [1/2" x 1" x 58'] cut in 27 pieces of varying lengths
WM 123 half round [5/16" x 5/8" x 30'] cut in 14 pieces of varying lengths
LWM 248 stock [3/4" x 1-3/4"]

Bamboo on walls:
WM 120 half round [1/2" x 1" x 435'] cut in lengths from 7' to 8'
WM 123 half round [5/16" x 5/8" x 435'] cut in lengths from 7' to 8'
WM 248 S4S [3/4" x 1-3/4" x 108"] cut in 2", 3", and 4" lengths

Other:
Ply-Bead® or Bedford Village® pre-finished wood paneling
1 pair wooden interior shutters
Oak finish wood stain
Latex paint
Bamboo poles for headboard and footboard
1/4" plywood for awning
3d or 4d finish nails
Hammer
Wood glue
Tape measure (preferably 25' rule)
Goggles

Getting Started

First paint the room a deep teal or "jungle" green with a good quality flat or semi-gloss latex paint. Then outline the grass at the base and top of the room with a pencil. Let the children paint the lower grass while you paint along the ceiling, using a lighter green than the walls.

Next frame the backboard of the bed using a 5' x 7' piece of Georgia-Pacific Ply-Bead® or Bedford Village® pre-finished real wood panels. Use 7' bamboo poles on either side of the paneling. You may be able to find bamboo poles at an import shop or through a store that sells rattan furniture.

The footboard for the bed was created by using two large pieces of bamboo, cut 22" high, for the ends. Then nail two pieces of bamboo on the diagonal to the ends. The footboard is connected to the headboard by two 6'-long sideboards made of 1" x 6", which may be painted or stained.

To make the "bamboo" on the bed's awning, alternate 1" and 1/2" half rounds (here Georgia-Pacific WM 120 and WM 123). Cut the half rounds into lengths varying from 22" to 26". To make the bamboo look realistic, use a 1/2" half round about every third shoot. Attach the half rounds to the plywood canopy with wood glue and finishing nails. Note: If half rounds are unavailable, you can piece together two quarter rounds for the same effect. Stain the "bamboo shoots" with an oil-based oak stain.

The "bamboo" canopy over the bed is a 1/4" piece of plywood cut 18" deep x 5' wide and installed at a 45-degree angle. The top of the canopy is secured to a strip of 1" x 2" stock, which is nailed to the wall. The decorative bamboo braces (out of real bamboo pole) are approximately 18" long, bottom cut on a 45-degree angle. These may be glued and nailed with 4d finish nails to the wall.

24

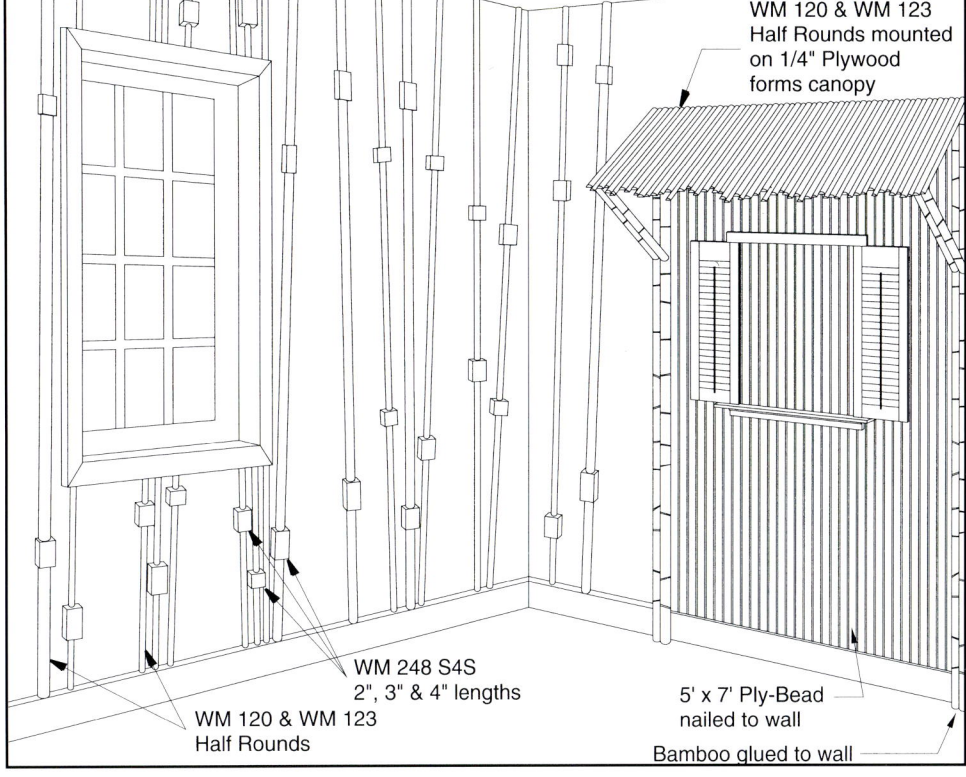

WM 120 & WM 123 Half Rounds mounted on 1/4" Plywood forms canopy

WM 248 S4S 2", 3" & 4" lengths
WM 120 & WM 123 Half Rounds
5' x 7' Ply-Bead nailed to wall
Bamboo glued to wall

Framing the Tiger

The tiger poster over the bed was mounted directly to the wall with its own cardboard backing, just as it came from the store. WM 248 screen/S4S stock frames the tiger. A shelf was made at the bottom by using a 27" inch piece of WM 433 casing and a 24" piece of WM 248 S4S stock finished with WM 100 cove base. The 27" interior shutters were attached directly to the S4S stock, which frames the poster. Be certain to anchor the screen stock securely to studs or wallboard with appropriate hardware. (Because poster sizes vary, the S4S stock and casing should be cut to dimensions that will frame the poster size you have selected. The size of the shutter is also determined by the finished size of the poster and frame.)

The Bamboo Forest

The bamboo shoots around the room are made like those on the bed's awning. Stain the half rounds or quarter rounds and cluster 2 to 3 bamboo shoots per running foot, leaving 18" to 24" between clusters. Use two different thicknesses, such as 1" and 1/2" (WM 120 and WM 123). As before, use a 1/2" half round about every third shoot. Cut the half rounds at different lengths and at random intervals, add pieces of S4S stock (WM 248), cut in 2", 3", and 4" lengths for a bamboo look that might even fool Kipling.

An inexpensive bamboo-type window shade was purchased to finish off the jungle room.

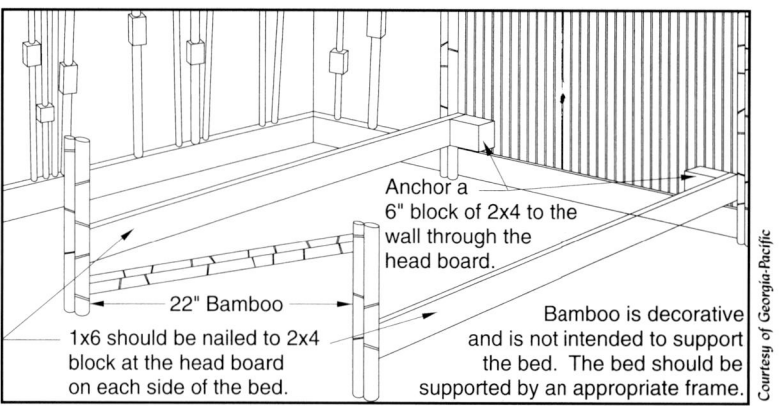
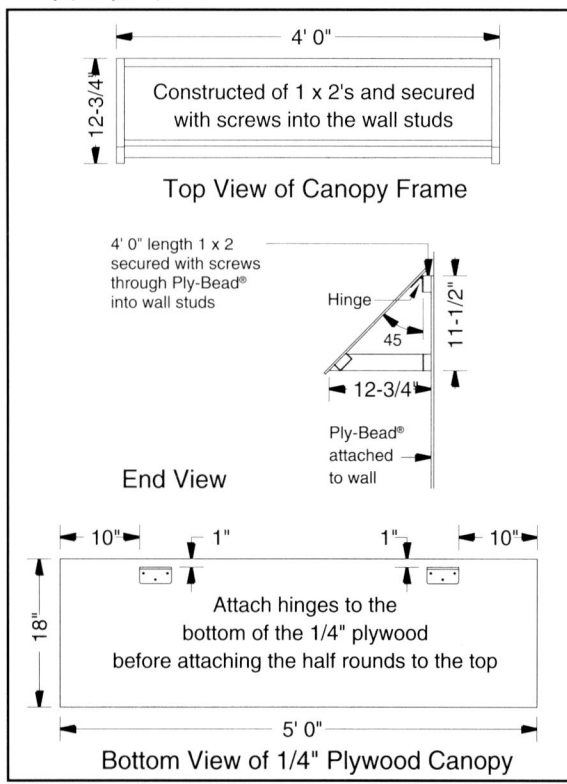
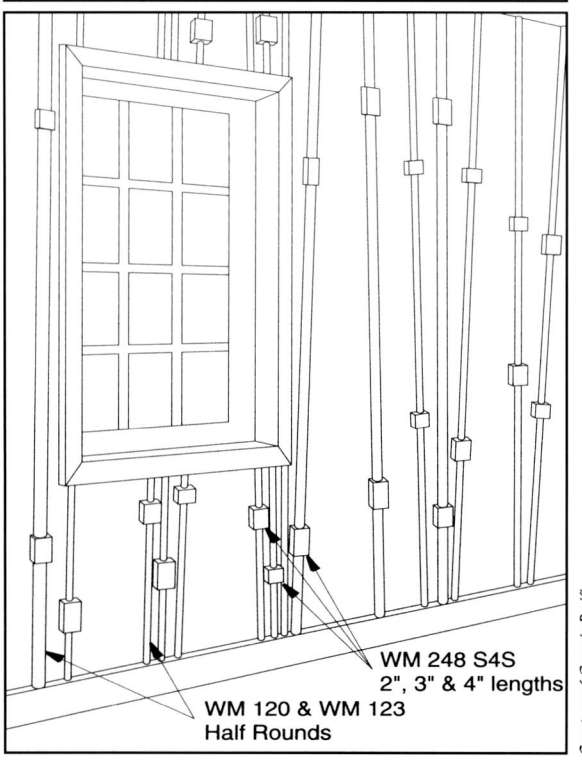
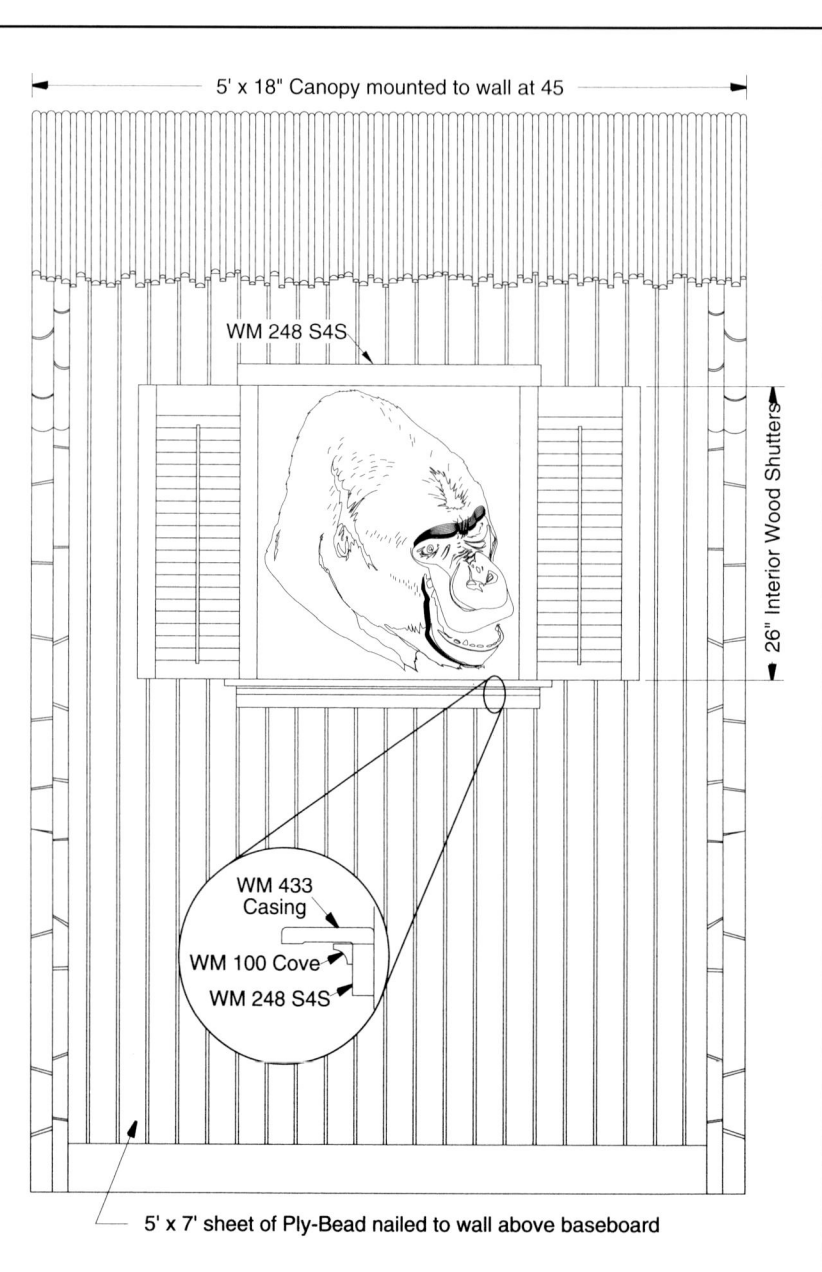

Formula One Room

Courtesy of Georgia-Pacific

Here's a bonding exercise for father and son, creating a room your child will want to race to at bedtime. This room has a 9' ceiling and a twin bed, but you can customize the design to fit the particular dimensions of your child's room.

Materials Needed

WM 248 S4S [3/4" x 1-3/4" x room measurements]
WM 937 stop [7/16" x 11/16" x room measurements]
WM 129 base [7/16" x 11/16" x room measurements]
WM 137 shelf edge [3/8" x 3/4" x 42']
WM 281 back band [11/16" x 1-1/8" x 17']
WM 163 base cap [11/16" x 1-3/8" x 10']
WM 292 ply cap [9/16" x 1-1/8" x 17']
LWM 233
LWM 266
WM 233 full round [1-5/16" x 2"]
WM 248 S4S for raceway [3/4" x 1-3/4" x room measurements]
WM 100 cove [11/16" x 11/16" x 10']
WM 230 handrail [1-1/2" x 1-11/16" x 15']
WM 248 S4S tire trim [3/4" x 1-3/4" x 17']
1/4" plywood and 1' x 4' for the signs and toy box
3/4" plywood and flex-board for the tires
Primer/sealer
Matte latex or semi-gloss latex enamel
Bandsaw or jigsaw
3d (1-1/4") or 4d (1-1/2") finish nails
Hammer
Tape measure (preferably 25' rule)
Wood glue
Hinges for the toy box

Vertical Roadway

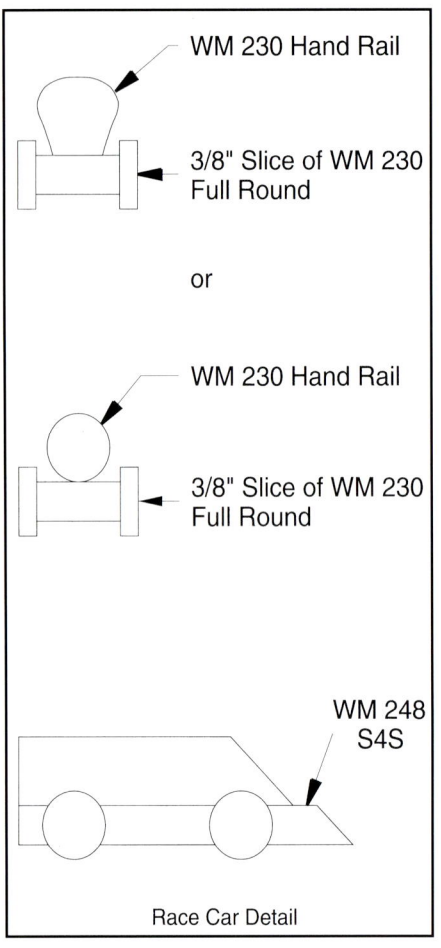

Race Car Detail

Courtesy of Georgia-Pacific

Start the project by determining how far from the top of the wall you want the molding to begin. The molding outlines the "roadway" around the top and down one side of the room.

Here we began 18" from the top of the 9' ceiling and used Georgia-Pacific's WM 248 S4S stock finished with WM 937 stop molding on one side and WM 129 base shoe on the other. The roadway was painted using a matte finish, dark blue latex, and the molding is painted with white latex.

You can make a line of yellow wooden cards going up the wall, or simply cut and paint blocks of lumber to resemble a dotted yellow line in the road. If you want to create your own fleet of cars, use a material, such as Georgia-Pacific's WM 230 handrail, cut 8" long with a 45-degree angle on the front to make the chassis. Cut round dowels (full rounds) into four cylinders, 1/2" thick, for the tires and paint them black. These wheels were made from WM 233 full rounds (1-5/15" diameter dowels). Glue the car together with a high-quality wood glue. Then anchor a narrow S4S stock (WM 248) to the wall and glue the cars to the S4S stock.

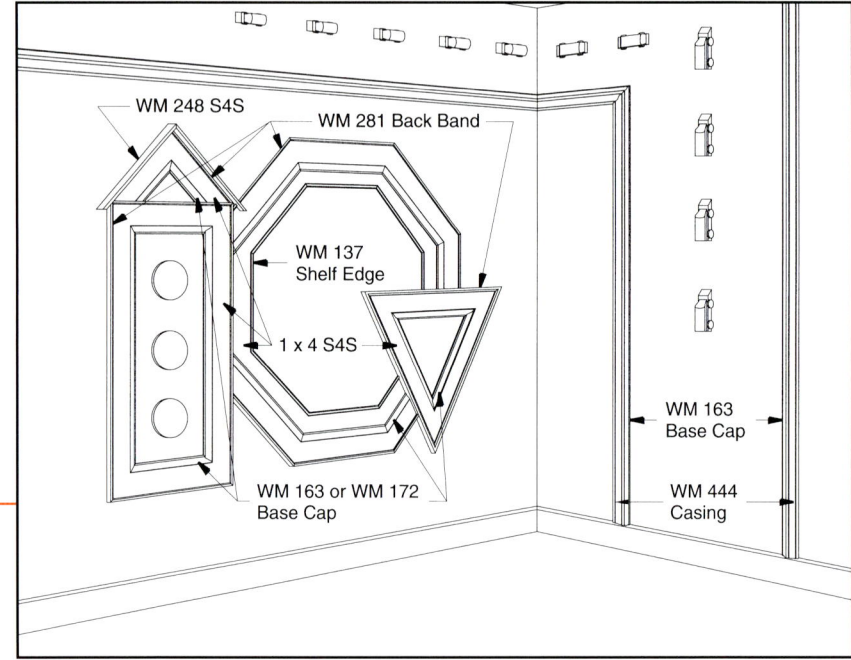

Courtesy of Georgia-Pacific

The Signs

The borders of the signs are formed of 1" x 4"s and were attached directly to the wall with finish nails and then painted. The molding creates an outline for each sign, which is then painted once in place. The Stop sign was made first, and measures 24" outside from point to point with the eight sides cut at a 22-1/2 degree angle. To make the inside octagon on the sign, use a thin edge molding (Georgia-Pacific's WM 137). All three signs are finished with a 1" x 4" to which a back band (WM 281) was applied. Next make the Yield sign, determining how far you want to be from the corner. The Yield sign is 36" outside from point to point; the triangle was made by cutting 60-degree angles. The inside triangle on the Yield sign and the inside rectangle of the Stop Light were made with Georgia-Pacific's WM 163 base cap. The final sign, the Stop Light, has a 36" high x 18" wide rectangular base with a 17-1/2" ply cap (LWM 266) attached.

The inside detail of the sign is WM 163 base cap. To make the "lights," trace three circles using a one-quart paint can as a template. Then use a bandsaw or jigsaw to cut the circles out of the wood. Glue the "lights" on the sign with wood glue.

Courtesy of Georgia-Pacific

The Toy Box

A toy box at the foot of the bed was fashioned from 1/4" plywood. Hinges at the top allow it to open and close. Be sure to purchase safety hinges that allow the toy box to close slowly. The toy box's dimensions are 13" high in front; 19" high in back; 36" wide and 18" deep. Draw an 18" line from the 13" front to the 19" back to determine the angle needed for the sides of the box and cut two pieces of plywood at this angle. WM 137 shelf edge molding and WM 100 cove are used for trim. The yellow oval "decal" on top is a free-hand design in latex paint. You may customize your toy box with numbers or colors as desired. The 24" freestanding tires beside the toy box were made with two 24" diameter circles cut from 3/4" plywood and a 6" wide piece of flex board. On the front of the tire, we cut a rim 4" from the edge. Use glue and finishing nails to attach the flex board to the 24" circles. You can make the tires any size you choose, however, be sure to allow for additional molding to trim the tires if they are larger than 24". Molding on the wheel is LWM 233 and WM 137 shelf edge.

For a much similar look, but a simpler project, you might substitute a painted plywood circle. The same moldings can be applied to resemble spokes on the wheel.

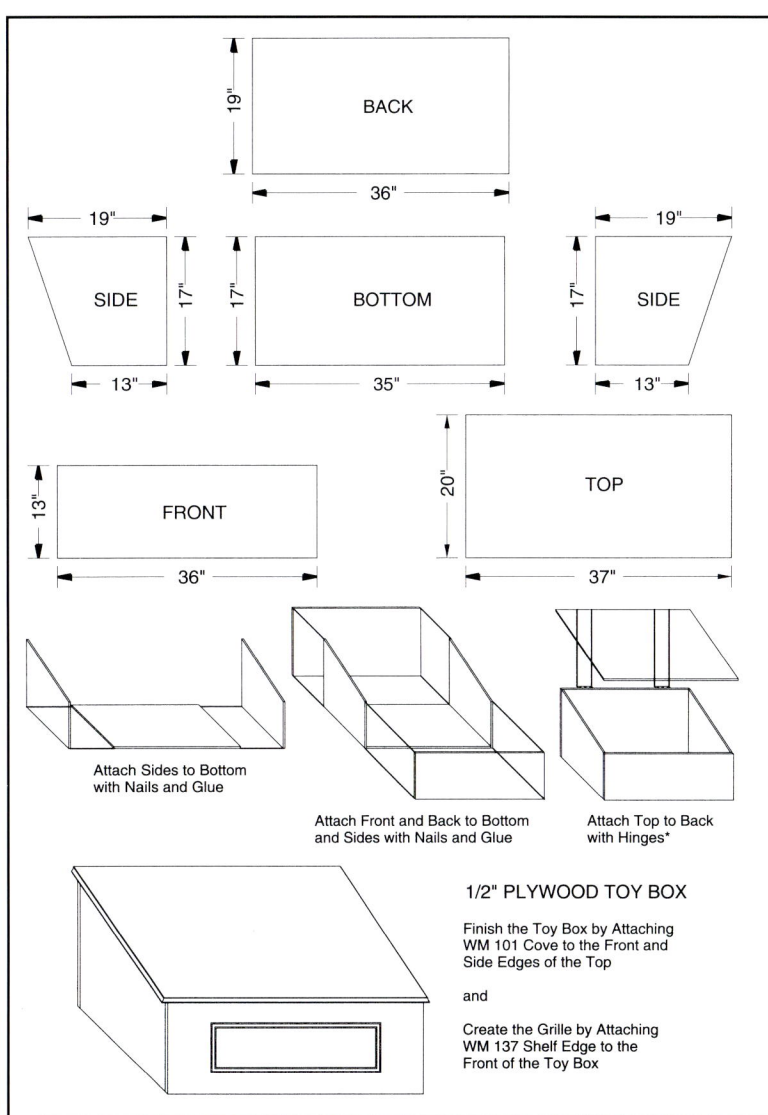

Courtesy of Georgia-Pacific

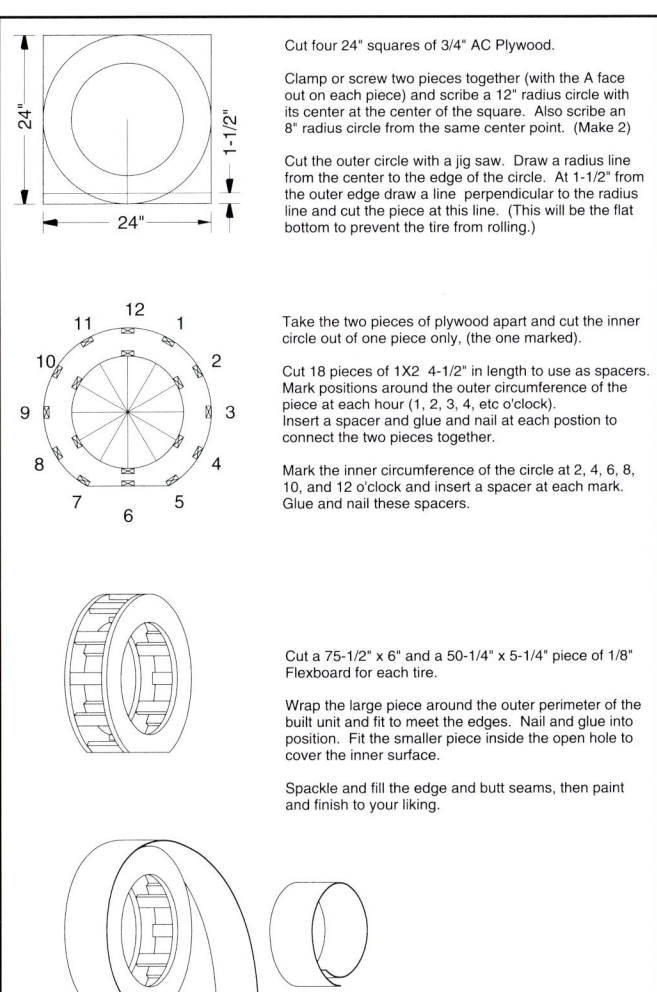

Cut four 24" squares of 3/4" AC Plywood.

Clamp or screw two pieces together (with the A face out on each piece) and scribe a 12" radius circle with its center at the center of the square. Also scribe an 8" radius circle from the same center point. (Make 2)

Cut the outer circle with a jig saw. Draw a radius line from the center to the edge of the circle. At 1-1/2" from the outer edge draw a line perpendicular to the radius line and cut the piece at this line. (This will be the flat bottom to prevent the tire from rolling.)

Take the two pieces of plywood apart and cut the inner circle out of one piece only, (the one marked).

Cut 18 pieces of 1X2 4-1/2" in length to use as spacers. Mark positions around the outer circumference of the piece at each hour (1, 2, 3, 4, etc o'clock). Insert a spacer and glue and nail at each postion to connect the two pieces together.

Mark the inner circumference of the circle at 2, 4, 6, 8, 10, and 12 o'clock and insert a spacer at each mark. Glue and nail these spacers.

Cut a 75-1/2" x 6" and a 50-1/4" x 5-1/4" piece of 1/8" Flexboard for each tire.

Wrap the large piece around the outer perimeter of the built unit and fit to meet the edges. Nail and glue into position. Fit the smaller piece inside the open hole to cover the inner surface.

Spackle and fill the edge and butt seams, then paint and finish to your liking.

Before moving on, please fasten your seat belts!

Bringing Baby

This has to be the most exciting moment in the life of a family – baby's arrival home. So much thought and care go into preparing for this moment, with less than nine months to make sure that everything is absolutely perfect.

In all the preparations, don't forget to take pictures. Baby won't actually remember his or her nursery, and a parent's memory may fail as well. Be sure to take the time, when the sun is shining in brightly, to take some snapshots of the room for baby's book. For your book, too! This, after all, is where you take the first precious steps toward getting to know one of the most influential people in your life!

Denim blues and white unite in cheerful and timeless contrast. *Courtesy of Waverly, a division of F. Schumacher & Co.*

These proud parents prepared for their little girl with solid rock maple furniture she'll use until she passes it on to grandchildren. *Courtesy of Moosehead Mfg. Co.*

Home

Pink and white mark this pretty room the domain of a new princess. Stripes and gingham plaid create blocks of color, bordered with floral accents. *Courtesy of Waverly, a division of F. Schumacher & Co.*

Wallpaper can be both pretty and educational – here providing a jump-start on the alphabet. *Courtesy of Waverly, a division of F. Schumacher & Co.*

Opposite page: A dreamy sky blue with puffy clouds is the theme of this hand-painted furniture, set against a sunny yellow background. Courtesy of *What's A Mother To Do?*

Colorful wallhangings, border paper, and linens define this baby's new world. *Courtesy of Moosehead Mfg. Co.*

Biblical beginnings are reflecting in this nursery theme, where Noah's ark lands on a dry mountaintop, and animals parade two by two.
Courtesy of What's A Mother To Do?

Neutral tones in the furnishings – green and ivory with hand-applied, burnished gold leaf — can be accessorized with blue or pink when the gender of the new occupant is discovered.
Courtesy of What's A Mother To Do?

Doctor
Tuesday 10:00
What's A MOTHER to Do?
7 lb.
21 inches
Call Mother!
to xo
Once upon a time
Happily ever after
DESITIN

White and yellow furnishings include tromp l'oeil treatments, eye-fooling bows and tassels that add catchy punctuation to this softly colored environment. Courtesy of *What's A Mother To Do?*

Circus themes are a historical favorite in the nursery. *Courtesy of What's A Mother To Do?*

A plastic tree and a jungle border are early inspirations for tropical dreams. For the baby who has everything, this little nursery set is loaded with places to pack it, including drawers beside and below the crib. *Courtesy of Berg Furniture*

An early 1900s color scheme creates a sentimental room, seemingly furnished with antiques while providing the latest in comfort, storage capacity, and safety. *Courtesy of Berg Furniture*

What serves as a changing table now may later work to display a television, a bouquet of flowers, or a birdcage. Wooden cabinets will be useful for decades to come, in any capacity the homeowner chooses. *Courtesy of Berg Furniture*

Innocence and timelessness are evoked with whites and pale pastels. An alphabet border unifies the colors and creates a focal point where parent and child meet halfway. *Courtesy of Eisenhart Wallcoverings Co.*

A mélange of stars and moons creates the background for a cheerful blue and yellow theme in this nursery. *Courtesy of Eisenhart Wallcoverings Co.*

Expecting twins, mom chose a soft palette of greens and white, soothing colors suitable to either sex. Her creative treatment incorporates a bubbles and waves motif. *Courtesy of The Glidden Company*

Photographer – John Gruen/stylist – Amy Leonard

Photographer – John Gruen/stylist – Amy Leonard

45

A newborn enters the world in pure white furnishings, with a welcome from tried-and-true antiques. *Courtesy of Lexington Home Brands*

This nursery enjoys the luxury of space, and thus the parents were able to invest in furnishings that will last the child a lifetime. *Courtesy of Bassett Furniture*

Nursery rhymes adorn an infant's furnishings, including a big clock complete with mice running up and down its sides. *Courtesy of Bassett Furniture*

Rag rugs and colorful quilting work with the country styling of the furnishings for an old-fashioned nursery. Chicken and rooster art are sure to delight the little one, and farmyard antiques will delight the grandparents. *Courtesy of Bassett Furniture*

Cheerful teddy bears await a new addition to this blue and yellow room, where it's unknown whether the new occupant is a boy or a girl. *Courtesy of Bassett Furniture*

An old blanket rack holds this baby's pastel warmers, and antique toys and clothing create a wonderful past where baby can put together his earliest memories while mother reminisces. *Courtesy of Bassett Furniture*

A precious new arrival is sheltered under the eaves, with warm wood and wicker tones to soothe the eyes, soft brown teddies to squeeze. *Courtesy of Bassett Furniture*

His Room

Deep blue dreams are hatched in this colorful corner, where wainscoting creates an underwater world. Cutouts on the Spartan blue bed frame and the wall above unify the theme. *Courtesy of Village, a brand of FSC Wallcoverings*

Tool chests and gas station memorabilia, an aviator poster and wallpaper border, and a model plane were used to personalize a boy's room. *Courtesy of Village, a brand of FSC Wallcoverings*

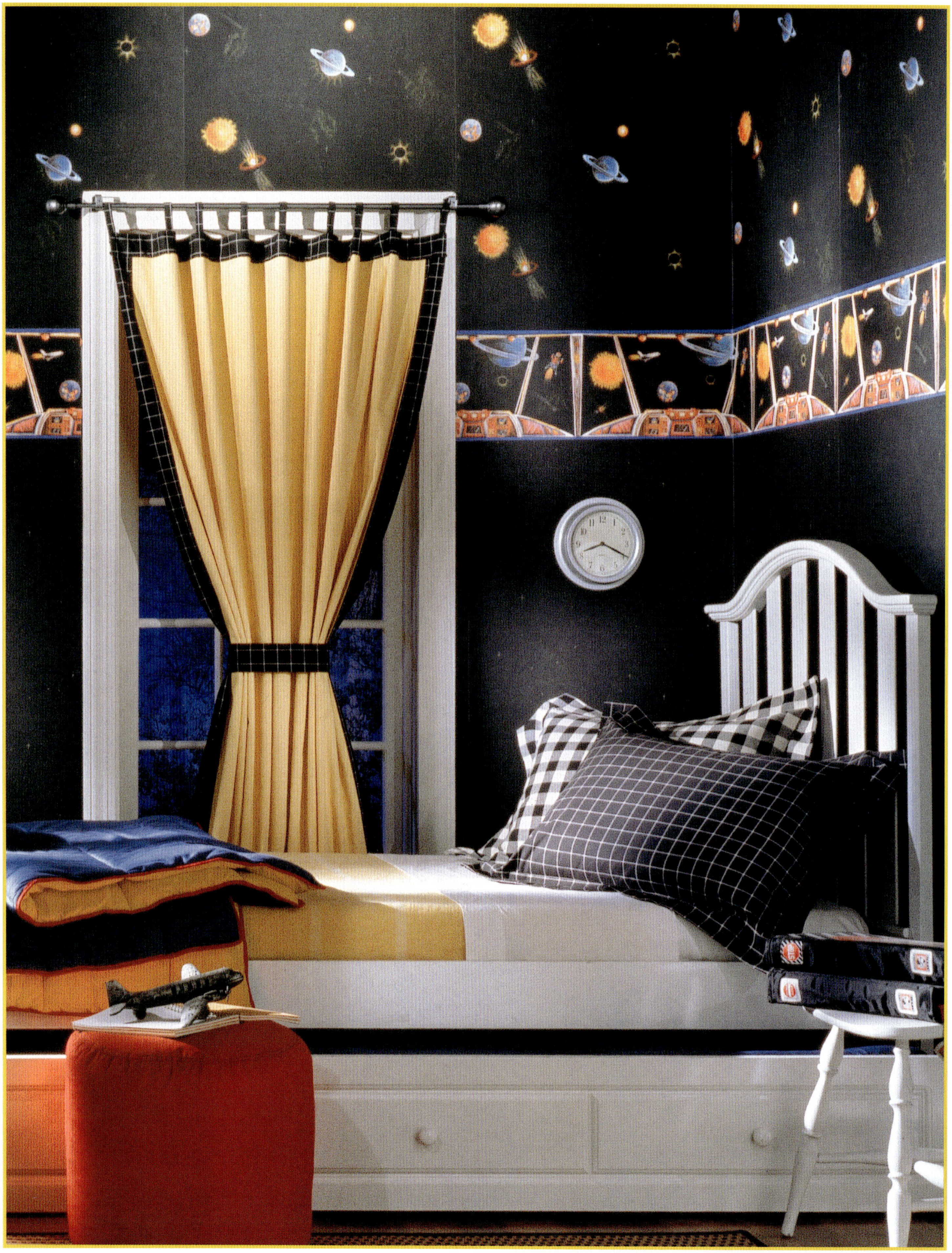

Bright, primary colors are generously layered in this boy's room. A propensity toward things that go "zoom" is reflected in the wallpaper motifs. *Courtesy of Village, a brand of FSC Wallcoverings*

Opposite page: Midnight black gains celestial highlights from planetary wallpaper pattern and contrasting white on the window and bed frames. *Courtesy of Waverly, a division of F. Schumacher & Co.*

A wall unit doubles as dresser, desk, and display unit. *Courtesy of Moosehead Mfg. Co.*

53

Bright bedding on stackable bunk beds adds cheer to a small room for two. *Courtesy of Berg Furniture*

Neutral wood furnishings and painted walls allow for a quick makeover whenever the occupant desires. *Courtesy of Sandberg Furniture*

Here's a lucky boy, with lots of drawers where he can hide things away, or stuff it quickly when his mother tells him to clean up. *Courtesy of Sandberg Furniture*

Besides establishing a national identity, red, white and blue make for a stunning color theme. Here an antique finish adds interest. *Courtesy of What's A Mother To Do?*

Dramatic contrasts were created with a slate green wall, bright white furnishings, and a rainbow of bright accent colors. *Courtesy of Vermont Precision Woodworks*

Red and black accents add masculinity to a room warm and neutral in wood tones. *Courtesy of Vermont Precision Woodworks*

A bed becomes a fort, complete with slide-out desk, and lots of drawers and cubbyholes where things tuck away. *Courtesy of Gautier USA, Inc.*

56

Space artist Robert McCall designed this border – a Tour of the Universe™ – that stretches nearly fourteen feet before repeating itself. Most borders repeat every twelve inches. *Courtesy of Eisenhart Wallcoverings Co.*

A sail completes the effect in this fantasy bed for young buccaneers. The prow doubles as display shelves, and cabinetry under the sleeping quarters allows for storage. Very cool! *Courtesy of Gautier USA, Inc.*

57

Red is an exciting accent color in interior design, and here it has been used liberally. It works well to tone down the daily effect of scattered children's toys. *Courtesy of Riverside Furniture*

Mix and match twins stack for space-saving effect, and the head and footboards have been alternated to create variety in the arrangement. Courtesy of Fashion Bed Group

Fire trucks and fire dogs adorn a bed for a future station chief. Courtesy of Fashion Bed Group

Wrought iron gets contemporary flair in this arching design, in a room that makes use of timeless whites and blues. *Courtesy of Fashion Bed Group*

Wrought iron rails allow lots of light in and around this bunk bed; an important asset in a room where space or the perception of it, is at a premium. *Courtesy of Fashion Bed Group*

Sailors salute in a room that's all boy. Boat and plane cutouts tie these charming maple furnishings into the theme. *Courtesy of Fashion Bed Group*

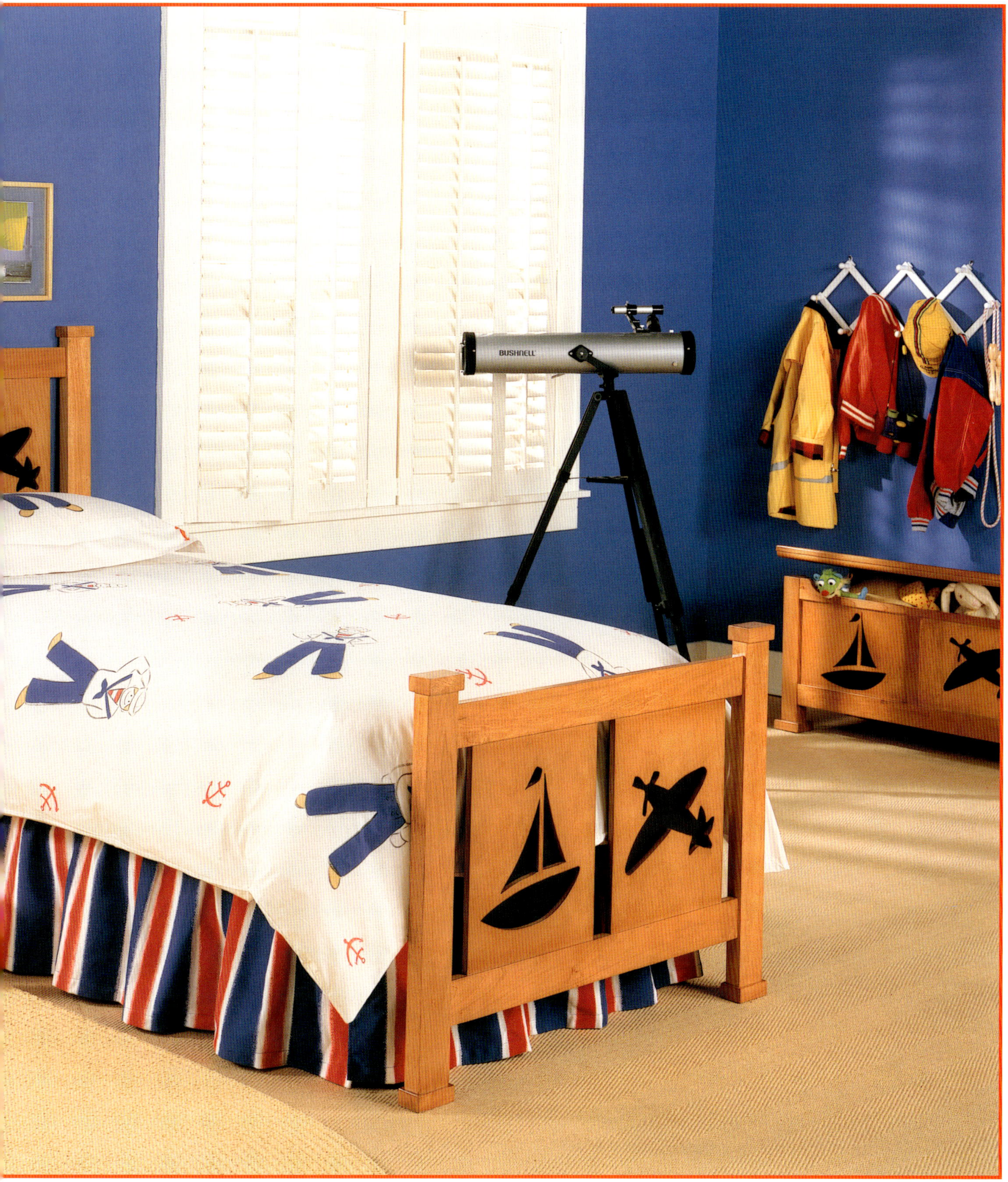
BUSHNELL

Photographer – Keith Scott Morton/stylist – Amy Leonard

By painting old furniture to match, pieces look like they were made for each other. And the whole room becomes more coordinated. *Courtesy of The Glidden Company*

Photographer – Keith Scott Morton/stylist – Amy Leonard

Rich golden contrasts add cheer in tones of Tender Rose, Corn Silk, and Sand Dune. *Courtesy of The Glidden Company*

A decorative stripe outlines doors and window, and creates a sky where pinwheels hang suspended. *Courtesy of The Glidden Company*

Two beds, a desk, and a dresser become one, very cool, integrated unit in this compact bedroom set. *Courtesy of I.D. Kids*

Bright bedding allows "vroom vroom" play to continue long after lights out. *Courtesy of Dan River, Inc./Oliveira Brandwein Design, Inc.*

Simplicity can be so exciting, here in the brilliant blue and white contrast of painted furniture. *Courtesy of Maine Cottage*

Opposite page, bottom left: **It's rush hour in a room full of things that go "vroom." The green theme makes it easy on decorators, while an intense concentration of vehicles unleashes a child's imagination.** *Courtesy of California Kids*

A toddler's toys compete for sleeping space. *Courtesy of Lexington Home Brands*

©Oliveira Brandwein Design, Inc.

This kid sleeps with bed bugs, a theme carried throughout the bed linens. The homeowner continued the theme on the walls and furniture with hand-painted insects and snails. *Courtesy of California Kids*

A boy's toys are stashed below, or they're supposed to be, when not in use. *Courtesy of Lexington Home Brands*

This boy's bedroom is the quiet retreat he needs to get his homework done. Courtesy of Moosehead Mfg. Co.

A small room looks smart with simple, elegant furnishings. *Courtesy of Berg Furniture*

Who says bunk beds should be stacked parallel? This configuration creates a cave-like getaway below, complete with shelving and a reading light. It also allows for drawers and a desk. *Courtesy of Berg Furniture*

A small room is maximized by raising the bed and packing storage space below. A pullout stepladder allows access to this mid-level bunk. *Courtesy of Berg Furniture*

Stackable bunk beds and modular dresser and shelf units allow for an endless variety of configurations; a perfect strategy for adapting to new family members or new houses. *Courtesy of Berg Furniture*

Boys multiplied can raise cane here, with bunk space for three on sleepover night. *Courtesy of Vermont Precision Woodworks*

A rollout bed provides a comfy place to sleep by night, and tucks away to leave lots of floor space to play by day. *Courtesy of Gautier USA, Inc.*

A super futuristic effect is achieved with silver and gray tones. A very cool retreat for a sci-fi fan. *Courtesy of Gautier USA, Inc.*

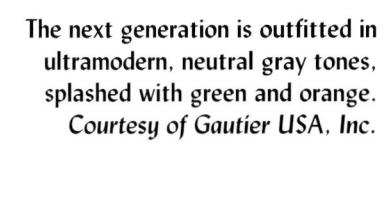

The next generation is outfitted in ultramodern, neutral gray tones, splashed with green and orange. *Courtesy of Gautier USA, Inc.*

A desk swings out or tucks away under the bed, one of many solutions created with modular furnishings. *Courtesy of Gautier USA, Inc.*

Red, white, and blue denim with a fish motif make for an exciting room. Courtesy of Aubergine Home Collection, Inc.

Bottom left: Steel blue laminates are accented by natural wood in contemporary furnishings. Yellow accents add warmth. Courtesy of Gautier USA, Inc.

Bottom center: A big soccer ball bolster and pillow are great for play on or off the bed. Sports accessories make this a boy's room, but the theme could be changed in an afternoon with a quick trip to a department store. Courtesy of P.J. Kids

Opposite page, bottom right: Far-out design teaches a child that the sky is no limit, with an inspiring space border and clouds above. Courtesy of Eisenhart Wallcoverings Co.

A fantasy in fiberglass, this jungle hideaway is right out of a children's fairytale. *Courtesy of Creative Arts Unlimited, Inc.*

Nautical red, white, and blue is an enduring and endearing theme in children's decor. *Courtesy of My Room*

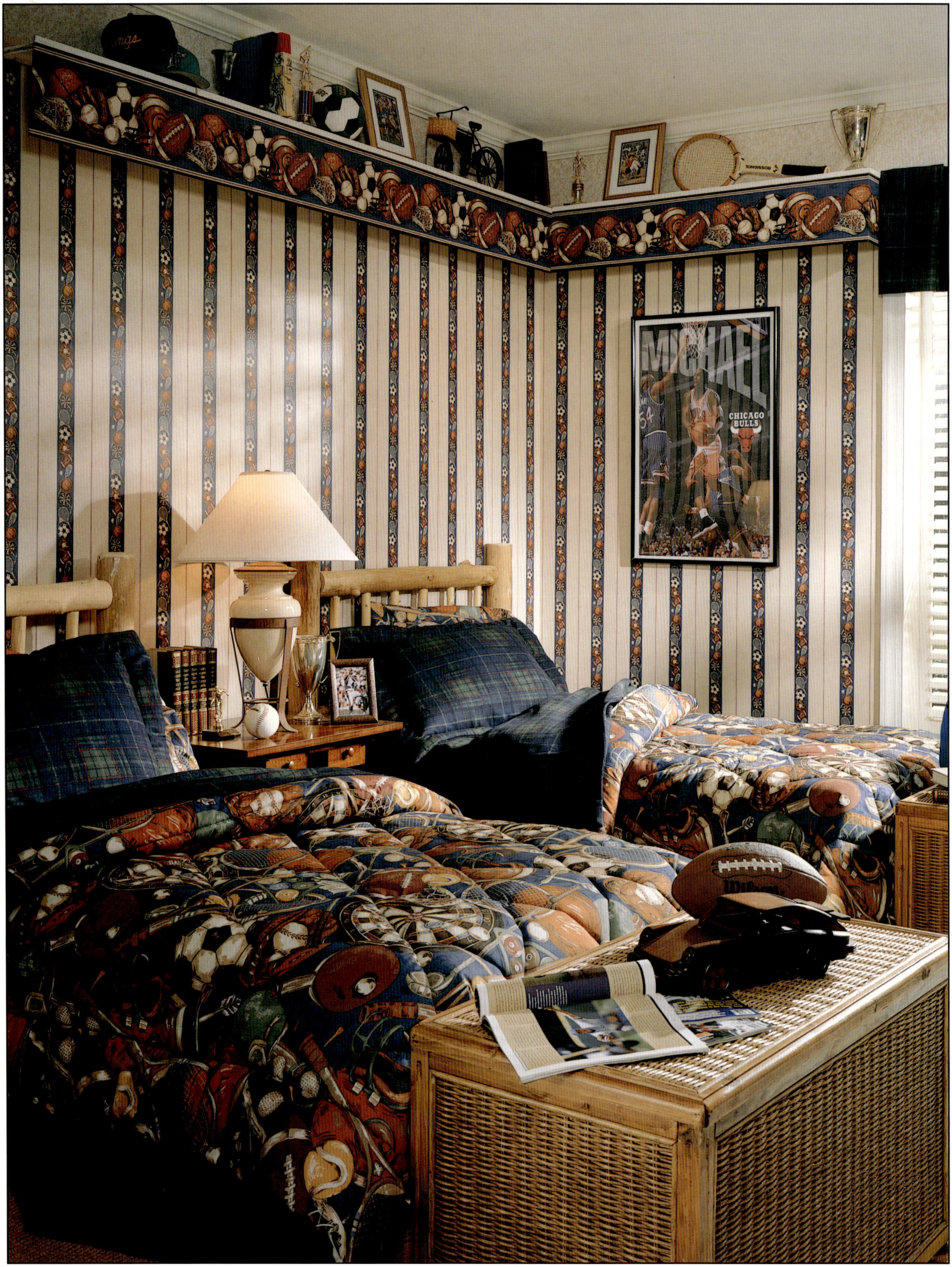
MICHAEL
CHICAGO BULLS

An outdoorsman enjoys his own entrance, a great way to sneak in the day's specimens without making mom squeamish. She's obviously indulgent, though, having framed floral and faunal finds on an aptly themed wallpaper. *Courtesy of Eisenhart Wallcoverings Co.*

Expensive cars, fast computers, and a place for sports trophies – this room is dressed for a son's success. *Courtesy of Eisenhart Wallcoverings Co.*

Opposite page: A high-up shelf is a great way to stash the clutter, here underlined by a sports theme wallpaper border that ties in with bedspreads. *Courtesy of Eisenhart Wallcoverings Co.*

A nautical theme includes cream walls and furniture the color of a midnight sea, rendering the room restful. *Courtesy of Riverside Furniture*

Far-out space adventure takes place right here, against an aubergine and gold backdrop. *Courtesy of The Glidden Company*

76

77

Sleeping space doubles as a cool fort, with above, below, and inside places to clamber. After all, a bedroom chamber isn't just for sleeping. *Courtesy of I.D. Kids*

A young champ's space is outfitted like a locker room. *Courtesy of I.D. Kids*

For the kid who has everything, here are places to put it. Modular furnishings create tons of storage space in both dressers and as part of integrated shelving and under the bed drawers. *Courtesy of I.D. Kids*

A young man's varied interests are reflected in his room, souvenirs of his past and tools of his future. *Courtesy of Lexington Home Brands*

An electronic scoreboard is the highlight of this sports lover's abode, and what's even cooler — it works. His cabinetry is configured like lockers, only rich in wood grain. Note that there are no table lamps set out to break, and there's lots of motivation to keep things stored away in order to use the basketball hoop. *Courtesy of Lexington Home Brands*

A rollout bed can accommodate an overnight teammate. *Courtesy of Lexington Home Brands*

Shelving and storage flanking the bed can easily be reconfigured to a new room. *Courtesy of Lexington Home Brands*

Paneling and wood furnishings lend rustic air to a room that sleeps three. *Courtesy of Lexington Home Brands*

Two brothers bunking up can make for a mess, but you've got to expect that. *Courtesy of Lexington Home Brands*

Bold colors create excitement combined with country-style furnishings. *Courtesy of Lexington Home Brands*

Cutouts in the headboard and the armoire create the illusion of tall pines, adding to the rustic feel of this loft bedroom. *Courtesy of Lexington Home Brands*

81

Creator David Shayne Laro likes to recreate objects in enormous excess of their original size. Here a huge hammer sheds light on a dresser that resembles a stack of giant books, and nearby scissors steady a table. An enormous fishhook on the wall has bagged an action figure, while another readies to dial 911 on a large-print keypad that doubles as headboard in a very imaginative bedroom. *Courtesy of David Shayne Laro*

GBH Studios, West Lebanon, NH

Below: It's not hard to guess what these boys are doing on any given Sunday! Big fans, they've got related bedding and accessories as their primary decor. *Courtesy of Dan River, Inc./NFLP*

©2000, National Football League

82

A bench and shelves were built-in to the footboard of this bed, a rollaway bed tucked behind it. *Courtesy of Lexington Home Brands*

Nautical motifs adorn a boy's blue room, adding a patriotic decorative touch to classic wood furnishings. *Courtesy of Lexington Home Brands*

Her Room

A jungle themed wallpaper is easily complimented by natural tones in paint and textiles. The effect comes to life with a few stuffed animals. *Courtesy of Waverly, a division of F. Schumacher & Co.*

Dream-like pastels were used for little girl's fantasy retreat. *Courtesy of Village, a brand of FSC Wallcoverings*

A dollhouse unit contains clothes, toys, and a television for a living doll. Courtesy of What's A Mother To Do?

86

Opposite page: Big sister is an honored guest in this little girl's room. A trundle bed is for friends when they're allowed to sleep over. Courtesy of Moosehead Mfg. Co.

A wallpaper divide defines upper and lower territories in a room built for two young siblings. *Courtesy of Sandberg Furniture*

A princess's palace comes with plenty of room to pirouette and pretend. *Courtesy of Vermont Precision Woodworks*

Pink flowers and lace were hand painted on furniture to fashion this little, feminine retreat. *Courtesy of P.J. Kids*

©1999 Greg Wilson Studios

A colorful Harlequin pattern in 3-D and swoop tops were carved from wood in this fantastic bedroom ensemble. *Courtesy of Creative Arts Unlimited, Inc.*

A castle is created around a bed, part of a princess's fairytale kingdom. *Courtesy of P.J. Kids*

A Noah's Ark theme works perfectly for a young child who adores stuffed animals. *Courtesy of Eisenhart Wallcoverings Co.*

Tucked in a tower, in her parent's gorgeous new castle of concrete, a young girl enjoys a fairytale retreat. *Courtesy of Essroc Cement Corp./The Watier Family*

Photographer – Jeff McNamara/stylist – D.J. Carey

Pretty pinks gang up for a very girlish room – a terrific toddler's retreat.
Courtesy of The Glidden Company

Photographer – Jeff McNamara/stylist – D.J. Carey

Zalewa Image Designers, Georgetown, IN

Pink and green perfect the *prima donna's* place. Courtesy of The Glidden Company

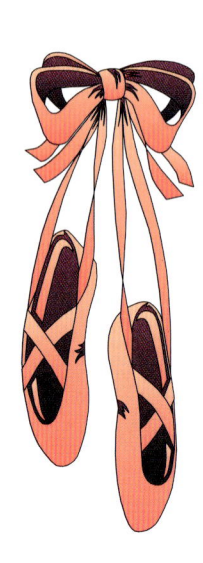

Basic white laminate finishes will endure years of use, and work with any chosen color theme. *Courtesy of I.D. Kids*

Sweet pinks adorn white furnishings in a little girl's room, set atop a wonderful painted wood floor. *Courtesy of I.D. Kids*

Soft chenille and lacey cutouts in the woodwork combine for feminine effect in this eclectic room. *Courtesy of Maine Cottage*

Twin princesses each rule, with beds of their own, and shelving too. *Courtesy of Lexington Home Brands*

Turquoise and white create a crystal clear room, where blue accents stun. *Courtesy of Lexington Home Brands*

Sugar and spice make everything nice, like white on white with sprinkles of pink. *Courtesy of Lexington Home Brands*

Blue and white, from the lace curtains to the painted floorboards, to the very foot of a sleigh bed create a remarkably pretty room. *Courtesy of Lexington Home Brands*

A hand-painted wall mural adds fairytale excitement to this lovely little girl's room. She dreams of princes and dragons on a fluffy bed of white. *Courtesy of Lexington Home Brands*

White furnishings create contrast in a dormer room of pastel green, blues, and purple. *Courtesy of Lexington Home Brands*

©Oliveira Brandwein Design, Inc.

A few accessories and a colorful comforter create a Wild West corral. *Courtesy of Dan River, Inc./Oliveira Brandwein Design, Inc.*

A dancer's accouterments define the Barbie® Ribbon Ballerina comforter, and an incredibly popular young girl's fantasy. *Courtesy of Dan River, Inc./Mattel, Inc.*

Pastels create a pretty place. Here lavender, green, and yellow work together to define a young girl's space. *Courtesy of Waverly, a division of F. Schumacher & Co.*

Antique furnishings are unified in one room by artfully matched florals in the wallpaper and linens. *Courtesy of Waverly, a division of F. Schumacher & Co.*

98

Flowers make it feminine for a young lady who's very conscious of beauty. *Courtesy of Moosehead Mfg. Co.*

Modular units are unified by a blue countertop that wraps this room and provides lots of work and display space. Additional storage is tucked under the bed.
Courtesy of Berg Furniture

A botanist's dream, bugs and buds punctuate this soft, garden-theme room. *Courtesy of What's A Mother To Do?*

Nestled amidst floor-to-ceiling cabinetry, this princess enjoys an economical castle constructed from modular units. *Courtesy of Berg Furniture*

The outdoors comes in with wonderful landscape scenes hand painted on the furniture. *Courtesy of What's A Mother To Do?*

Modular furniture allows for the most from a small room, wrapping the walls in storage space. Dust bunnies have been displaced by a pullout drawer under the bed. *Courtesy of Berg Furniture*

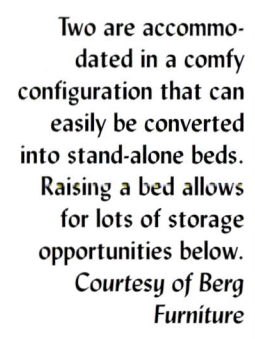

Two are accommodated in a comfy configuration that can easily be converted into stand-alone beds. Raising a bed allows for lots of storage opportunities below. *Courtesy of Berg Furniture*

On one side a vanity and media unit, on the other a study area. Color coordinated surface tops and knobs were used to customize this room for a little girl, and are as easily changed as her tastes and interests. *Courtesy of Berg Furniture*

Classic furniture styling creates a beautiful room, easily redecorated to adapt to the age and tastes of its occupant. *Courtesy of Berg Furniture*

Here's a room guaranteed to draw approval from grandmothers. A sweet floral spread and soft yellows make this a sentimental room for someone's little sweetheart. *Courtesy of Berg Furniture*

Pretty pastel pinks accentuate the feminine in this young woman's boudoir. *Courtesy of Sandberg Furniture*

A canopy is a wonderful fantasy element for a room, perfect for princesses. Here cutout hearts create a unifying theme in natural-finish pine furniture. *Courtesy of Sandberg Furniture*

Solid cherry wood accents were incorporated in the head and footboards as well as the tops and knobs on a modular storage and shelving unit. *Courtesy of Vermont Precision Woodworks*

Splashes of color create excitement among simple, elegant furnishings. *Courtesy of Vermont Precision Woodworks*

A staircase complete with handrail makes for safe climbing to the upper bunk. It also creates shelves and nooks for creative storage. *Courtesy of Gautier USA, Inc.*

This room is punctuated with primary colors, including an inexpensive bouquet of foam swimming "noodles." *Courtesy of Gautier USA, Inc.*

Manufacturers are breaking away from traditional wood-tones, providing bright paint finishes on the furnishings. The result is a bold and cheerful room. *Courtesy of My Room*

106

Blue accessories and door fronts add mod flair to this room, where twins were stacked to sleep two. *Courtesy of P.J. Kids*

Bright colors create a festive room that's fun to hang out in. *Courtesy of My Room*

Stylized rose petals create a pretty pink pattern on bedroom and play furniture. *Courtesy of P.J. Kids*

Simple furnishings allow a child to come in with their favorite toys and personalize a room. *Courtesy of P.J. Kids*

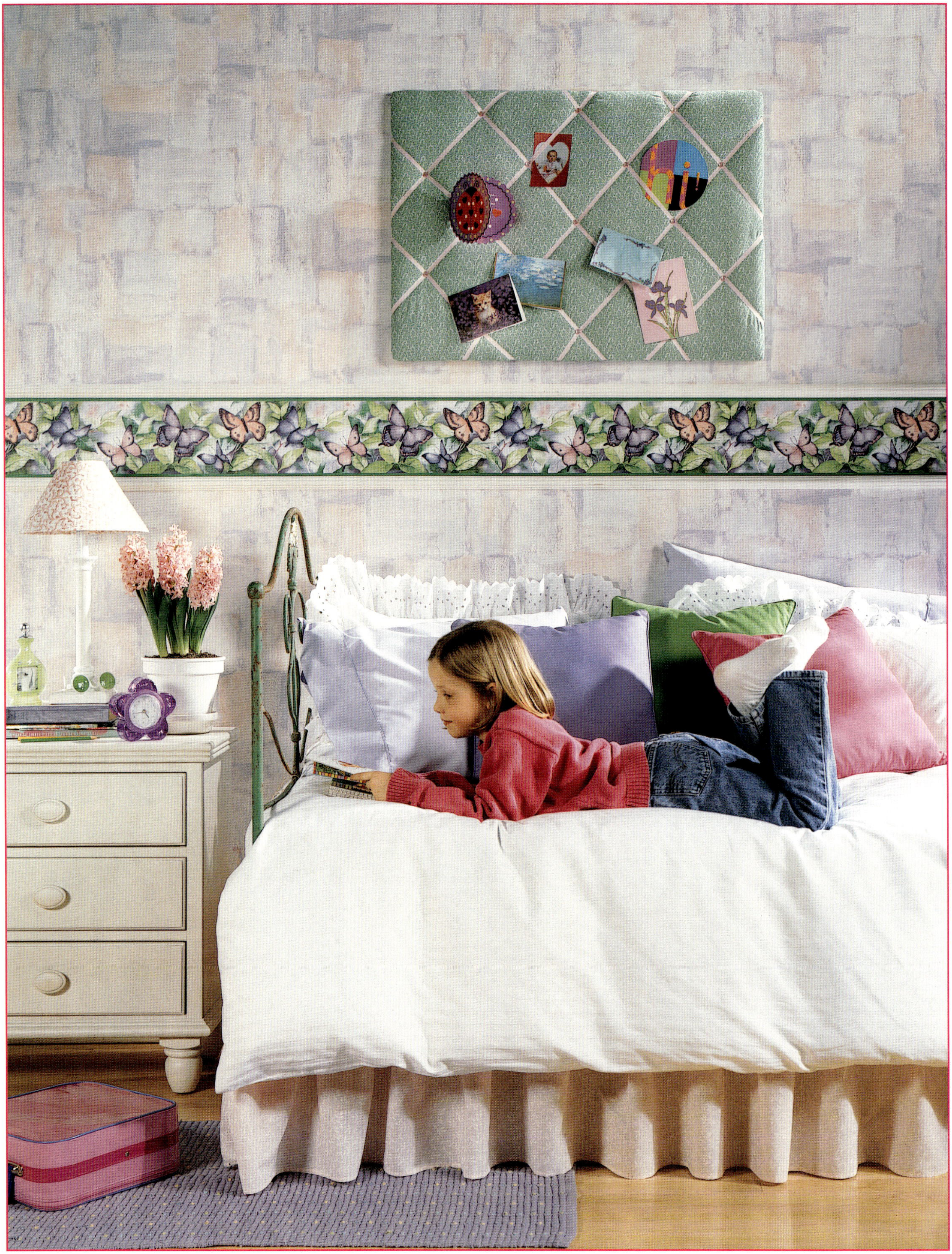

California artist Jodi Jensen created this wildflower garden design for the walls. White linens and picket-fence woodwork complete the theme. *Courtesy of Eisenhart Wallcoverings Co.*

Every girl loves flowers, and here the room is replete with them, from the framed blooms to the garden wallpaper designed by California artist Jodi Jensen. *Courtesy of Eisenhart Wallcoverings Co.*

Opposite page: A quilted bulletin board is a great way to display the latest pinups in a room as pretty as the occupant. *Courtesy of Eisenhart Wallcoverings Co.*

109

Neutral furnishings in classic styling work with cheerful yellow walls to create a blank palette where favorite accent colors can shine. *Courtesy of Riverside Furniture*

Not all children are inclined to clutter. A neat and tidy girl keeps her bed made just so, her books stacked neatly. She enjoys wrought iron furniture in an antique white finish. *Courtesy of Fashion Bed Group*

A courtly motif arrays royalty on a bright bedspread, underlined by a bright skirt to add feminine flair. *Courtesy of Fashion Bed Group*

Pink linens and prints match in this pretty girl's bedroom set. Pink and yellow buds color-key with wall and rug. *Courtesy of I.D. Kids*

© 1999 Scott Dorrance

Classical styling and neutral colors – natural wood and white – will allow this room to mature for decades to come. *Courtesy of Vermont Tubbs, Inc.*

Hot colors in textiles and paint brighten this exciting room, accented by whites. *Courtesy of Fashion Bed Group*

Photographer — Jeff McNamara/stylist — D.J. Carey

A young girl gets the "hip" room she requests. Mom asked her to collect toys, paper, ribbons, and candy that reflected her favorite colors, and then to narrow the search by picking two as the main colors, two for accents. The result is blue on blue, with lemon and lime for flavor. *Courtesy of The Glidden Company*

Photographer — Jeff McNamara/stylist — D.J. Carey

Bright basics adorn this cheerful room, personalized with bunches of wood-cut flowers. A footboard on the bed adds a swoosh of style, and color keys with tops on the dresser and desk. *Courtesy of I.D. Kids*

A bunk not only doubles up on sleeping space but also on storage – a big drawer underneath is a great place to stash winter linens or seasonal clothes. *Courtesy of I.D. Kids*

Stunning contrast in deep purple and white furnishings add excitement to this room. *Courtesy of I.D. Kids*

Putting the furniture on wheels allows this young lady to rearrange her little room whenever she likes. *Courtesy of Maine Cottage*

114

A glorious four-poster bed stands amid footed furnishings in this feminine boudoir. *Courtesy of Lexington Home Brands*

A girl's pretty purple room is at the ready for a spur-of-the-moment sleepover. *Courtesy of Lexington Home Brands*

Bright colors open up a little girl's room, making it a draw day or night. *Courtesy of Lexington Home Brands*

Great accents were added in pink and lavender paints and textiles to feminize classic wood furnishings. *Courtesy of Lexington Home Brands*

Mixing pink patterns creates a snug and secure feeling in this sweet little guest room. *Courtesy of Lexington Home Brands*

Fancy white furnishings suit a young lady who likes things just so. Here she demonstrates her decorative flair with millinery displays. *Courtesy of Lexington Home Brands*

A little girl shares her digs with lots of critters. With a pullout bed and an upper bunk, there's always room for friends, too. *Courtesy of Lexington Home Brands*

An active young lady is growing up amidst furnishings chosen to mature with her. *Courtesy of Lexington Home Brands*

Laces and delicate fabrics feminize furnishings, all finished in a wonderful antique white for a feeling of timelessness. *Courtesy of Lexington Home Brands*

Jungle animals parade through bright purple and yellow tones, corralled by a hand-painted border that ties the room together. *Courtesy of California Kids*

Pretty rose buds punctuate soft pink stripes in this decidedly feminine abode, complete with a ruffled canopy over the bed and a bright bow on the lamp. *Courtesy of California Kids*

Pretty lilac tones adorn this room top to bottom, from the lining of a lace canopy over the bed, to the sheen on a painted wood floor. *Courtesy of California Kids*

Heart-shaped pillow, a heart-shaped stool, and plenty of pink hearts printed everywhere express the loving sentiments that went into this room's decor. *Courtesy of California Kids*

118

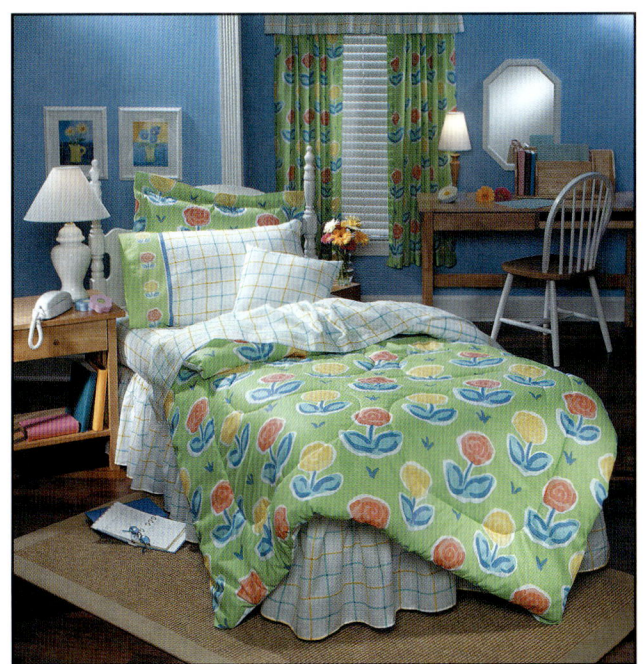

Color creates excitement in this room, with lime green textiles against a baby blue wall. *Courtesy of Dan River, Inc./Di Lewis Studios*

This room is full of far-out flowers for a very cool girl. *Courtesy of Dan River, Inc.*

Buds and birdhouses cap a cheerful gingham bed skirt in this bright abode. *Courtesy of Dan River, Inc./Oliveira Brandwein Design, Inc.*

Clouds drift by Victorian-styled white furnishings, a fantasy effect in a very feminine room. *Courtesy of Lexington Home Brands*

119

You're Always

Photographer — Jeff McNamara/stylists – Amy Leonard & Ingrid Leess

Welcome

Ribbons seem to suspend two pretty pictures above a flock of little friends in the wallpaper border. *Courtesy of Eisenhart Wallcoverings Co.*

Color coordinating linens and paints enliven a room, here in a refreshing palette of mint and blues. *Courtesy of The Glidden Company*

Top left: It works as a couch or a daybed for a little visitor, and there's a pullout bed below, too. *Courtesy of Lexington Home Brands*

Opposite page, center: A young guest uses a basket of extra pillows to get comfortable with as she helps prepares for a party. *Courtesy of Lexington Home Brands*

Opposite page, bottom left: Two pretty beds, all in a row: a sentimental room awaits the laughter of visiting grandchildren. *Courtesy of Lexington Home Brands*

Above: A palette of blues and lavender stripe whites in this pretty, soothing room. *Courtesy of The Glidden Company*

A picket-fence bed lends itself to a garden theme, and is easily accessorized. *Courtesy of Fashion Bed Group*

Red, white, and blue are popular decorator themes throughout the home. In this bedroom it gives a distinctively boy atmosphere. *Courtesy of Sandberg Furniture*

A plant lover has stashed toys in this room, a lure to delightful little visitors. *Courtesy of Sandberg Furniture*

125

When you buy good furnishings for your children's room, you stand to lose – they're going to ask to take them away when they move! *Courtesy of Vermont Precision Woodworks*

Hand-painted furniture adds a touch of whimsy to a room rich in textiles. An inviting window seat beckons, and a stepstool helps a child climb up into a big, soft bed. *Courtesy of Julian Katera, Inc. Interior Design*

A mix of colors, of old and new, creates a sentimental retreat. *Courtesy of Julian Katera, Inc. Interior Design*

Netting and lace reflect a grandmother's taste. Old-fashioned, fancy turned work on the bed makes it a future heirloom. *Courtesy of Lexington Home Brands*

Here are some of mommy's favorite things, preserved in a pretty room by a loving grandma for special trips to "I remember when." *Courtesy of Lexington Home Brands*

A canopied bed, shuttered windows, and a sentimental collection of toys and books create a magical bedroom. *Courtesy of Lexington Home Brands*

The craftsmanship of yesteryear creates classic styling for contemporary furnishings. The effect is completed with layers of lace and pastel print textiles. *Courtesy of Lexington Home Brands*

Who wouldn't want to come back after staying in a cool room like this? Bright colors, games, and good books make this a fun place to be, for kids of any age. *Courtesy of Maine Cottage*

Indestructible furnishings and toys are at the ready for ever-welcome young visitors. *Courtesy of Maine Cottage*

128

Neutral blue accents make this room an appropriate place for any grandchild, and a comfortable spare room for storing grandmother's sewing and craft supplies. *Courtesy of Gautier USA, Inc.*

Old-fashioned taste is reflected in grandma's spare room, where Colonial inspirations style the new furniture, accented by antiques. *Courtesy of Lexington Home Brands*

After a beloved daughter moves out, her room stays filled with sentimental memories. Mother comes here to remember, and to await the grandchildren. *Courtesy of Lexington Home Brands*

Weekend Retreats

Traditional bunk beds are outfitted for him or her, a children's room in a weekend retreat. *Courtesy of Berg Furniture*

A great way to accommodate overnight guests is with a tuck-away bed. When not in use, it does a great job of blocking dust bunnies. *Courtesy of Vermont Tubbs, Inc.*

©1999 Scott Dorrance

Opposite page: A popular child can accommodate two friends on mini vacations without breaking out the sleeping bags. Courtesy of Vermont Tubbs, Inc.

Twins share a room and a desk. Simple furnishings can help clarify solutions to complex sharing issues. *Courtesy of Vermont Tubbs, Inc.*

©1999 Scott Dorrance

Children get their own room in a mountain retreat. Cutouts and color individualize the beds. *Courtesy of Maine Cottage*

A weekend home at the lake frequently plays hosts to little friends, so a rollout bed comes in handy. *Courtesy of Maine Cottage*

Red and white, day and night, this room with its fanciful painted furniture and warm quilts is a wonderful place to curl up with a good book. *Courtesy of Maine Cottage*

A guest room is ready to sleep four on demand. *Courtesy of Lexington Home Brands*

Here's bunking up in patriotic style. *Courtesy of Lexington Home Brands*

Rich wood finish and deep-lake blues epitomize the room of an outdoorsman. *Courtesy of Lexington Home Brands*

Rustic furniture and fishing accoutrements adorn this boy's den. *Courtesy of Lexington Home Brands*

Playrooms

Wonderful wallpaper motifs are plentiful and perfect for a play space. Here a propensity toward things that go "zoom" is reflected in the choice of motif. *Courtesy of Village, a brand of FSC Wallcoverings*

A rough and tumble cowboy has his room outfitted for Wild West fun. *Courtesy of P.J. Kids*

Children are starting young these days, and it's only appropriate that they have a computer station set up that's ergonomically correct. Primary colors make this children's furniture universally appealing. *Courtesy of P.J. Kids*

A tea party theme sets the stage for a game of imagination that has delighted generations of young girls. *Courtesy of P.J. Kids*

Drawing, coloring, stacking blocks, piecing puzzles together – these are the fundamentals of early learning. Children's play areas should accommodate and encourage these activities. *Courtesy of P.J. Kids*

Every child is a star. *Courtesy of P.J. Kids*

Bright colors create a cheerful playroom, a setting where fun is the obvious objective.
Courtesy of The Glidden Company

Photographer – Monica Buck/stylist – Amy Leonard

A super assortment of primary colors makes this family's rec room a stimulating place to play.
Courtesy of The Glidden Company

140

141

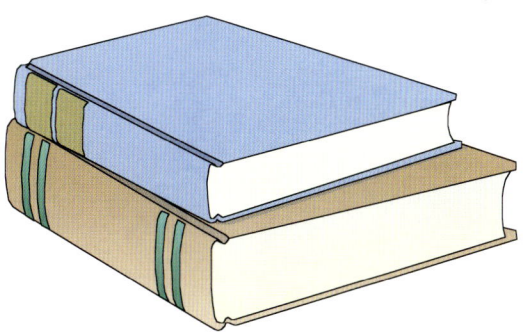

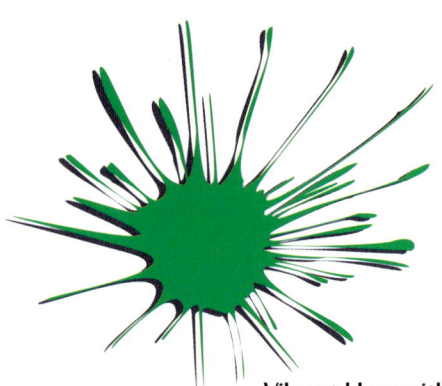

Vibrant blues with orange accents set the stage for fun and creative study. *Courtesy of Maine Cottage*

Tuffet-like stools invite Miss Muffets to belly up to a tea party, or some coloring, or whatever else their imaginations might concoct. *Courtesy of Maine Cottage*

142

Resource Guide

Aubergine Home Collection, Inc.
77 Wentworth Street Ste. 4
Charleston, SC 29401
843-722-3838
Founded in 1996, the company specializes in custom, high-quality bedding manufactured in the United States.

Bassett Furniture Industries, Inc.
PO Box 626
Bassett, VA 24055
540-629-6450
www.bassettfurniture.com
A leading manufacturer and marketer of branded home furnishings. Bassett's products provide quality, style, and value, are sold through Bassett Furniture Direct™ stores, At Home with Bassett®, and other stores.

Berg Furniture
28 Evans Terminal
Hillside, NJ 07205
908-354-5252
www.bergfurniture.com
This company specializes in children's furniture, including convertible crib/beds, modular units, and changeable countertops, knobs and other accessories that make it easy to customize a child's room.

California Kids
1135 Industrial Road
San Carlos, CA 94070
650-637-9054

Creative Arts Unlimited, Inc.
3730 70th Avenue North
Pinellas Park, FL 33781
727-525-2066
www.creativeartsinc.com/www.caudesign.com
This creative studio serves the retail industry, providing custom work for special promotions, unusual architectural fixtures and furnishings. Only the luckiest of children own their bedrooms.

Dan River, Inc.
1325 Avenue of the Americas
New York, NY 10019
800-223-7854
www.danriver.com
Among its diverse lines of textile products, the Home Fashions for Kids product line offers a complete assortment of fashionable juvenile bedding and accessories, and popular character licensed products.

David Shayne Laro
PO Box 1089
Quechee, VT 05059
802-296-2286
www.davidlaro.com
This woodworker collaborates with his inner child in designing fantasy furnishings, from spaghetti-full forks and big ballpoint pen lamps, to glass tables supported by Wild West pistols.

I.D.Kids
704 West Main Street
Teutopolis, IL 62467
217-540-3100
Dedicated to producing high quality youth furniture that is functional, safe, and sturdy, and designed to grow with the child within physical space confines and with changing color choices.

Eisenhart Wallcoverings Co.
P.O. Box 464
Hanover, PA 17331
800-931-9255
www.eisenhartwallcoverings.com
This company manufacturers a line of wallcoverings "Just for Kids," as well as borders, architectural elements, museum inspired designs, Arnold Palmer licensed designs, and other fine wallcovering products.

Fashion Bed Group
5950 West 51st Street
Chicago, IL 60638
800-825-5233
Fashion Bed Group, a Leggett & Platt Company, is part of the Ornamental Bed Division. They supply a large and innovative line of fashion beds, daybeds, futons, and bunk beds.

F. Schumacher & Co.
79 Madison Avenue
New York, NY 10016
800-423-5881
www.fschumacher.com; www.waverly.com
Founded in 1889, this privately held company supplies fine decorative fabrics, wallpapers, furnishings, and accessories, as well as bedroom ensembles, window treatments, and other home fashions.

FSC Wallcoverings
79 Madison Avenue
New York, NY 10016
800-423-5881
www.villagehome.com

Village brand products are carried through both independent and chain paint and wallpaper retailers, and are aimed at the first-time homeowner and do-it-yourselfer.

Gautier USA, Inc.
Copans Business Park
1521 W. Copans Road, Ste. 109
Pompano Beach, FL 33064
954-975-3303
www.gautierusa.com
French design in an entire range of easy living furniture for living rooms, bedrooms, nursery and offices. Available in 40 countries worldwide.

Georgia-Pacific
P.O. Box 105605
Atlanta, GA 30348-4706
1-800-Build-GP
www.georgia-pacific.com

The Glidden Company
925 Euclid Avenue
Cleveland, OH 44115
800-GLIDDEN
www.gliddenpaint.com
In addition to paint, this leading manufacturer of architectural paints provides decorating inspiration through their Glidden Color magazine, and color visualizer CD-ROM Color @ Home.

Julian Katera, Inc. Interior Design
622 Main Street
Avon-by-the-Sea, NJ 07717
732-897-8700

Lexington Home Brands
PO Box 1008
Lexington NC 27293-1008
800-539-4636
www.lexington.com
Offering furnishings for bedroom, dining, occasional, home entertainment, home office, and youth, plus wicker, upholstered, and leather seating, Lexington's many brand names include, Nautica Home, Bob Timberlake®, Tommy Bahama®, Betsy Cameron™, and Waverly®.

Maine Cottage Furniture Inc.
PO Box 935
Yarmouth, ME 04096
206-846-1430
www.mainecottage.com
This company offers simply styled home furnishings combining familiar architectural forms and vibrant colors. Maine Cottage specializes in producing high-end furniture that is fun and casual, too.

Moosehead Mfg. Co.
2 Monument Square
Dover-Foxcroft, ME 04426
207-997-3621
www.mooseheadfurniture.com
For nearly 60 years this family-owned company has produced heirloom quality furniture at affordable prices, fashioned from solid rock maple, ash, and birch and made with old-fashioned craftsmanship.

My Room, Inc.
8012 Westbury Drive
Warrenton, VA 20186
540-439-3966
www.myroomfurniture.com
My Room manufactures twin beds, bunk beds, trundle beds, dressers, night tables, desks, chairs, and toy boxes for the growing years.

P.J. Kids
306 Alexander Street
Princeton, NJ 08540
609-683-5437
www.pjkids.com
Founded in 1996, P.J. Kids, a leader in the children's home furnishings industry takes a lifestyle approach, offering a full array of floor pillows, rugs, ready-to-assemble furniture, upholstered, slip-covered, and foam seating, and case goods.

Riverside Furniture
PO Box 1427
Fort Smith, AR 72902
501-785-8263

Sandberg Furniture Mfg. Co., Inc.
P.O. Box 58291
Los Angeles, CA 90058
323-582-0711
www.sandbergfurniture.com
This company focuses on medium-priced bedroom furniture, finished with an extremely durable top coat, steel reinforcing brackets, and laminate and solid wood construction, making it ideal for children.

Vermont Precision Woodworks
249 Professional Drive
Morrisville, VT 05661
802-888-7974
www.vermontprecisionwoodworks.com
In the early 1980s this woodworking company recognized a niche in high quality children's furniture. Today they offer over twenty different bed styles and several case styles.

Vermont Tubbs Inc.
1 Tubbs Ave.
Brandon, VT 05733
802-247-3414
www.vermonttubbs.com
William F. Tubbs started steam-bending ash in 1840 to fashion snowshoes and skis. Today the company continues his tradition with enduring design, careful craftsmanship in their furniture manufacturing.

What's A Mother To Do?
PO Box 21252
Little Rock, AR 72221
888-WePaint
www.whatsamothertodo.com
Fine art meets fine furniture for children in this company's hand-painted pieces, all guaranteed to become family classics.